CULTIVATING HEALTHY MINDS:

A GUIDE TO MENTAL HEALTH RESOURCES VOLUME 1

FOR CHEFS AND HOSPITALITY INDIVIDUALS

BY COOKZCREED FOUNDATION

WWW.COOKZCREEDFOUNDATION.ORG

COPYRIGHT

Copyright © 2024 Cookzcreed Foundation

AUTHORS:
Kisha Washington
Cheryl C. Hill-Washington
Tiffany Washington Hudnall

All rights reserved. This book or any portion thereof may not be reproduced or used in any manner whatsoever without the express written permission of the publisher except for the use of brief quotations in a book review.

Printed in the United States of America

First Printing

ISBN
979-8-9909008-0-6

ADDRESS:
Winchester, VA

WEBSITE:
www.cookzcreedfoundation.org

INSPIRED IN LOVING MEMORY OF: SHAHEED CLAIBORNE

Who was Shaheed Claiborne...

Shaheed was a chef, artist, father, and friend, but most importantly, a human being who loved to help and support others in any way he could. He was from Baton Rouge, Louisiana, so the southern charm, and strength he exuded was second nature. His mom, a woman of leadership and fortitude gave Shaheed the pathway to be great in all aspects of his life. But, like so many others, Shaheed suffered from mental illness. On January 20th, 2020, Shaheed passed away just one week after the passing of his mother Betty Claiborne.

Some of Shaheed's Accolades include:
Top 10 Finalist at The World Food Championships
Burger/Brew Bash Winner
Owner of Booshay's Food Truck
Louisiana State Winner of Taste of America

DEDICATED TO FRIENDS AND FAMILY

Hill-Washington Family

To my mom (Cheryl) and sister (Tiffany) and the Hill-Washington Family, thank you for helping write this amazing book/guide. We have worked on this for a long time, and I'm so glad you all can see it to fruition. I would like to thank you as well for building this organization to its heights and where it's headed. The work we do in both the mental health field and culinary industry speaks volumes to who you both are and your character. So thank you for all you do… This book is for you!

Special Thanks to the Original Board:

Derek Williams
Khalid Rashadeen
Gerren Allen
Dwayne Rouse
Dave Overman
Tyler Hudnall
Terence Tomlin

Thank you to the original board members for believing in an organization to not only help ourselves through a tragic time, but to help and support others.

Cookzcreed Facebook Group
Mindful Chef Platform

DEDICATED TO FRIENDS AND FAMILY

To Arlina Hill

This book is dedicated you for being on the original team for all competitions. You have helped and supported Team TheKeyIngredient through The World Food Championships, Turn Up the Heat Gala, The National Capital Area Cake Show, and multiple others. You have truly seen the work that goes into working in the kitchen, being on the competition stage, and seeing the ups and downs of the culinary world. Thank you for your support.

To Dawn Helmedach

This book is dedicated to you with profound gratitude of your unwavering support and boundless kindness throughout the journey in the Mental Health industry. Your guidance has fortified the strength of others and illuminated the gravity of mental health in today's world. This book stands as a testament to our shared dedication and love, aimed at empowering every individual grappling with mental health challenges not just to survive, but to thrive." Thank you for your love and support!

DEDICATED TO FRIENDS AND FAMILY

To John Mattingly

John has been an amazing support through this journey. To the late night talks, to the research, to your service, I want to thank you. John is a MSgt Munitions Craftsmen Conventional Shop Chief with 26 years in the military and 7 deployments to Jordan, Iraq, Afghanistan, Saudi Arabia and Guam. Not only does he serve in the military, he has helped Chef Kisha compete in multiple competitions. He gets to see what the culinary world is all about. And, being in the military, sees first hand what military personal and veterans go through. Thank you, this book is for you.

To Juan Rich

Juan has been Chef Kisha's sous chef for years and gets an inside look into dealing with clients, fellow chefs and their stories. Juan has worked in the entertainment industry for 30+ years, doing events such as the A Different World College tour, sound engineer for BET, and Howard's Homecoming the last 24 years. With being Kisha's sous chef, Juan gets to see the ins and outs of mutiple events. Juan has been a huge support in this journey with on going conversations, talks of inner work and mental health, and how one gets better. Thank you, this book is for you.

ABOUT THE AUTHORS

Cookzcreed Foundation

MISSION:

We provide knowledgeable and sustainable resources for scholarships, mental health and substance abuse, and mentorship. We strategically and accurately provide these resources by working with our community, industry, and partners for chefs and hospitality individuals to achieve their goals and success.

Founder, Kisha Washington

Kisha Washington is the Executive Chef, Owner, and Founder of a personal/private chef business called TheKeyIngredient, llc and Cookzcreed Foundation. She is also a competition chef, as well as a mental health advocate. Self-Disclaimer: Kisha is not a licensed therapist, licensed counselor or doctor. She does however have certifications, training and over 15 years of extensive therapy and self-care practices.

Her accolades and affiliations include:

6 time Top 10 winner at The World Food Championships, Grand prize and 1st place at Riunite, and NCACS. Top 10 people's choice at Dessert Wars DC 2023, and 1st place people's choice at Culinary Fight Club New Orleans. She is an alum of the James Beard Foundation Legacy Network Program 2023-2024, a Member of The Mental Health Hospitality Coalition, Committee Member of the AFSP Virginia/Stephen City Chapter, Member of Just Call Me Chef, Judge for MD State Prostart and Prostart National Invitational with the National Restaurant Association, E.A.T certified judge and NRAEF scholarship judge. As well as certifications in Understanding Mental Health and Psychiatric Disorders, Understanding Behavior, Burnout, and Depression, Mental Health studies in Suicide, Violent Behavior and Substance Abuse, Applied Suicide Intervention Skills Training, and Healing Conversation Volunteer Training with the AFSP.

ABOUT THE AUTHORS

Cheryl Hill- Washington

Cheryl is the Chief Financial Director and VP Assistant for Cookzcreed Foundation. She has spent many years refining her craft. Helping others is one of her major strengths in the community and in her family. Cheryl has worked for a Mental Health Facility for 8 years and has found that she has learned something new about herself each day. Cheryl finds that helping in the organization the experiences are highly beneficial in helping herself to understand the procedures, rules, and regulations along with the growth of the company. She has a BA in Human Resources, and also a certification for judging food for the World Food Championships. Cheryl enjoys competing in competitions with the owner of Cookzcreed and expressing the creative craft in the food sport industry. She follows a motto: "Life Motivates Us to Change"! Because when life deals us an uncertain hand, you have to ask yourself what I am to do with this hand. I say be motivated and change! What about you?"

Tiffany Washington Hudnall

Tiffany is a director/ secretary in the Cookzcreed Foundation. She has years of experience working directly with individuals facing mental health and substance abuse challenges. She has recognized a pressing need for access to resources, support of patients, and teaching coping skills throughout ones life. Tiffany, in her daily efforts is dedicated to providing the groundwork to those in need of mental health assistance, driven by a profound commitment to others. Cookz Creed holds particular significance for her as it serves as a platform offering vital resources in mental health, financial stability, and education for members of the culinary community and beyond. Outside of her professional endeavors, Tiffany leads a fulfilling life as a parent to three beautiful children, being a creative through media, website building, and social media strategies, while balancing the demands of family with her career aspirations. Tiffany currently holds a BA degree in psychology and pursuing furthering her education. Tiffany is dedicated to expanding her capacity to support individuals in their journey toward mental wellness.

DISCLAIMER

Medical Disclaimer:

The information provided in this mental health and substance abuse resource guide/book is intended for general informational purposes only. It is not a substitute for professional medical advice, diagnosis, or treatment. Always seek the advice of your physician or qualified mental health provider with any questions you may have regarding a medical condition or mental health concern. The resources listed in this guide are not endorsements, and we do not guarantee the accuracy, completeness, or suitability of any information provided by external sources. It is essential to independently verify any information obtained from these resources and consult with a qualified professional before making decisions regarding your mental health or substance abuse treatment. We do not assume any liability for any direct, indirect, consequential, special, exemplary, or other damages that may result from reliance on the information provided in this guide or from the use of any resources listed herein. By accessing and using this resource guide, you agree to release us from any and all claims arising from or related to your use of the information provided. If you are experiencing a medical emergency, please call your local emergency services or go to the nearest emergency room immediately. Do not delay seeking medical or mental health treatment based on information obtained from this resource guide.

Organizations Disclaimer:

Cookzcreed Foundation is dedicated to promoting culinary excellence and sharing knowledge about, mental health, substance abuse, food and cooking. The content provided in this guide/book is based on the collective expertise and resources of multiple organizations and is their own research.

Chef Disclaimer:

The recipes, stories, and images featured in this guide/book are the creative work of the chefs affiliated with Cookzcreed Foundation. These materials are intended for personal use only and may not be reproduced, copied, or distributed without explicit permission from the respective chefs and Cookzcreed Foundation. Any unauthorized use of these materials is strictly prohibited.

HOW TO USE THIS BOOK/GUIDE

This is a guide/book for multiple resources. This is to help support you, get you on track, and get some inspiration or encouragement along this journey. This is not to replace getting actual therapy, counseling, or seeking medical help. If you feel you need medical help or are in crisis, please go to your nearest hospital or medical facility.

Through the state pages, you will find your state, along with state-level websites, as well as a community facility. *Note, facilities may not be directly near you. Please look at local facilities in your community. These facilities listed are 3 stars or more. Meaning people that have visited we able to locate and get information and/or support. Please make sure you are utilizing the state websites which have a lot of local and community information.

Next, you will find local resources to the DC, MD, and VA area since Cookzcreed Foundation is located in Northern Virginia. These websites and facilities have been recommended for this area, utilized in some way, or resources have been given out.

The next section of the book is for your particular interests. Websites, apps, techniques, self-care, Chef websites for equipment, etc. This is just to get you thinking of the items you may need to put in place. *Note, there are no affiliations with these websites, just recommendations on what has worked for chefs and hospitality individuals.

The last section of the book is our contributor section. Here you will find a PMHNP in practice, and organizations doing amazing work in the hospitality and culinary industry. Check out the programs and resources they offer in their various communities and websites. You will also find chefs, content creators, leaders, etc. They are doing awesome things in their culinary space, changing the culture of the kitchen, and sharing their stories of what it's like in the kitchen space. Follow them, show support, and connect.

CONTENTS

Introduction	1-2
Kisha Washington Story	3-6
Culinary/Hospitality Specific Mental Health and Substance Abuse Statistics	7-10
State Level Resources	11-26
Local to DC, MD, and VA	27
Websites, Apps, Self Care, Specific Items	28-41
Conclusion	42
Contributor Pages	
Bibliography	
Interactive Pages (Notes, Journaling, etc.)	

INTRODUCTION

"FOOD, A LOVE LANGUAGE"- KW

"TAKING CARE OF YOUR MENTAL HEALTH IS AN ACT OF SELFLOVE"- EH

Mental health in the culinary/hospitality industry goes unspoken, unsaid, and sometimes silenced. The challenges we face in our day-to-day interactions with customers, clients, employees, employers, mentors, and everyone in between have plagued our efforts to relish in the thing we love to do, which is create, cook, and tell our story through food. Some of the challenges include Burnout, Long Hours, Work and Family Balance, High-pressure environments, High Stress, Financial challenges, Physical strains, Mental strains, and much more...

We must address these challenges head on and see how we can help ourselves and each other by getting support, resources, or the things we need. Without these items in place, we continue the toxic cycle of suffering in silence, not taking care of ourselves, and having these things spill over into our personal lives, others, work, etc... So how can we be proactive in our mental health journey through the culinary industry?

We get proactive by setting ourselves up for success, by taking care of ourselves first. Our mental health, mindset, our thoughts dictate how we move about in the world. This guide/book will give you the first step of this journey. It will give you a glimpse at multiple levels of the steps to take for yourself.

At the end of the day, we want to start the conversation. A conversation of the real, a conversation of truth, a conversation that gets to the core of what we go through. This is the first step.

STARTING THE CONVERSATION

As a chef, we have thoughts running through our minds all the time. When we get to a certain point in our culinary journey or career, we look back and think, it took a lot to get to this point, what is next? where do I go from here? If there is one thing, I wish someone told me about the culinary/ hospitality industry before becoming a great cook then a chef, is that all the glitz and glam of cooking, does have its tradeoffs that go unexpressed. No one tells you about the late nights, going home to eat Ramen noodles or toast, after you fed these people a stunner of a multi-course dinner. Or the drive there to the restaurant, or a client's home, in traffic, hoping you aren't late, or didn't forget anything, and these people won't criticize each plate of food. Or the walk-in screaming moments and cries because the folks you are working with on the line just can't get it right, or you just got yelled at by the head chef or manager. No one talks about the intricate moments or thoughts, am I good enough? Why am I not getting ahead like I see everyone else doing? Why can't I move this business forward? How am I stuck at the restaurant with nowhere to go or flourish in my skills? Why don't people like my ideas or concepts? Is it me?

What do you do in these moments? When reflection clouds your mind, judgement of yourself, and you can't figure it out. What do you do when the ruminating thinking and talks to yourself become negative? Or the beratement of others, or your negative commentary turns into not feeling so good? The folks around you will tell you to brush it off, you're great, don't worry about what others say, you are amazing, you're the best... It's BS you're thinking. These people have no idea what I'm feeling, what my thoughts are, what I'm going through.

Or the imposter syndrome that we face. Or the jealousy or envy we feel from others. How about the stealing of intellectual property, or taking ideas, concepts from the very people we look up to, ride for, or are close to? Or the mental anguish you feel if you lose a Michelin star, or the sadness you carry when you have worked so hard and lose a competition, or you get that moment of finally opening a brick and mortar and something tragic happens like a fire, or someone steals your equipment or money has run out. Who supports you? Where do you go when the depression and sadness take your life over? When taking that drink, taking those pain killers, or holding these feelings in are no longer enough?

This is where the conversation starts: I need help with this. I need support in this journey. I need a listening ear. This, is the first step...

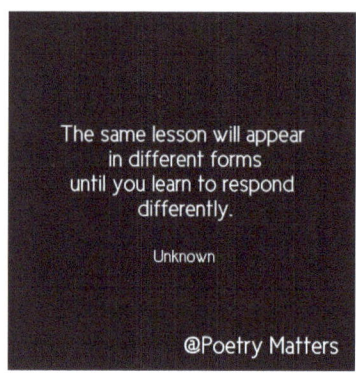

MY STORY

My story is a bit unique, marked by soaring highs and crushing lows, each phase leaving its mark. Mental health struggles have been a constant companion, moving through every facet of my existence. Anxiety, depression, self-harm, and the dark thoughts of suicidal ideations with 2 suicide attempts have shadowed my life, each being a painful reminder of my fragility. From the shattered dreams of a broken engagement to the grief of losing a close friend in 2017, I have weathered storms that threatened to engulf me in darkness. Yet, through it all, I have pressed on, walking my way back from the void time and time again. The lessons, hard-earned and bitterly won, have been etched into every part of my being, recurring with a relentless persistence that I could not ignore. Each trial, each setback, served as a teacher, driving home the importance of resilience and fortitude. Therapy became my haven, a place of solace and reflection where I wrestled with monsters both real and imagined. Yet, even as I explored the depths of my psyche, I came to realize that therapy was the beginning to the challenges that lay ahead of me.

Life, with its twists and turns, have a way of humbling even the most steadfast of individuals. Just when you think you have it all figured out, fate throws a curveball, forcing you to reassess and recalibrate. Yet, amongst the chaos and uncertainty, there is a glimmer of hope, a steadfast belief that each setback is merely a steppingstone on the path to self-discovery and growth. So, I press forward, with a newfound resolve and determination to confront whatever challenges that lie ahead, knowing that with each obstacle, I emerge stronger, wiser, and more resilient than before.

Food has entwined itself intricately into my life since I was a child. Memories flood back with every scent, every taste, binding me to cherished moments. I can still recall the comforting aromas that filled our home during Sunday dinners, the clatter of pots and pans as my mom cooked in the kitchen. Equally vivid are the images of my grandmother kneading dough for biscuits, infusing each one with a piece of her heart. Thanksgiving, holds a special place, where the delicious smells of my mom's paper bag turkey along with the scent of my aunt's sage-infused stuffing, creating an atmosphere of warmth and comfort. But it wasn't until a pivotal moment, a single day of discovery, that my passion for food truly ignited. In a sudden and unexpected twist of fate, I realized that the path of healthcare, once deemed inevitable, no longer resonated with where I wanted to go. Little did I know that this decision would set the stage for a journey back to my culinary roots, a journey that embraces me with an intensity I had never before experienced.

I enrolled in an advanced culinary arts and hospitality management program which felt like step into the career I wanted. Yet, as I delved deeper into the world of restaurant and kitchens, I found myself feeling a distaste with the demands of the industry. The grueling hours, the way it seemed to take over one's life, seemed at odds with my vision of a fulfilling career. And so, with unwavering determination, I set out on a new path, carving out a niche for myself in the realm of personal chef services.

MY STORY CONT.

In 2014, amid the hustle and bustle of my job at a doctor's office, TheKeyIngredient LLC was born, a self-expression of my culinary craft. But it wasn't until 2019 that I took the leap of faith to pursue my business full-time, embracing the title of entrepreneur. The reality of entrepreneurship, however, is far from glamorous. Behind the curtain of success lies a myriad of challenges, each one testing my intentions and pushing me to the brink of quitting. The endless juggle of client meetings and dinners, vendor negotiations, and marketing endeavors weigh heavy on my shoulders, leaving little room for interruption. Yet, it is in the quiet moments, the spaces between the chaos, that the true toll of this journey is felt. Driving home from a client's house, doubts and insecurities gnaw at the edges of my consciousness, whispering of inadequacy and failure. In a packed grocery store aisle, surrounded by endless possibilities, but my mind buzzes with worries and uncertainties. Budgets stretched thin, expectations unmet, the weight of responsibility bears down on me, threatening to suffocate my dreams in its unforgiving grip. And yet, in the dark silence of the night, I lie awake with only the glow of my phone for company, a voice rises from inside me. It is the voice of self-doubt, but also with confidence and conviction. Despite the apprehension that plagued me, despite the obstacles on my path, I am reminded of the passion that is within me, the flame of creativity that refuses to be extinguished.

For all the challenges, all the setbacks, there is a glimmer of hope, a light guiding me forward. And though the road may be long and uncertain, I walk forward. In the end, it is not the destination that defines us, but the journey itself, and the courage to pursue our dreams against all odds.

Throughout the journey of my life, food and cooking have been my stress relief outlet. There's something magical about the act of creating dishes that are not just nourishing but also whimsical, vibrant, and joyful. It's like painting with flavors and textures, and every meal becomes a canvas for self-expression and story telling. As I delved deeper into the culinary world, I found myself drawn to the exhilarating world of competition. However, what nobody prepared me for was the rollercoaster of emotions that accompany the highs of being victorious and the lows of losing. In the heat of the kitchen, amidst the pressure and scrutiny, I found myself questioning my identity and purpose. Am I cooking for the sake of artistry and authenticity, or am I merely chasing the validation of winning? The moments of anticipation before the judges' verdict became a battleground of nerves and hesitation. Yet, strangely enough, I found myself addicted to this adrenaline-fueled pursuit of excellence. It wasn't just about the trophies or accolades; it was about the undeniable drive to push boundaries and exceed expectations.

One of the pinnacle moments of my culinary journey came in 2019 when I clinched third place at the prestigious World Food Championships. The elation and sense of accomplishment were beyond words, made all the more special by the presence of my family and cherished partner. It was a moment of happiness, a culmination of years of hard work and dedication. But throughout the celebration, we pondered a deeper purpose – how could we use our platform to uplift others in the culinary community? What are the things chefs and those in the hospitality industry need on a day-to-day basis? Therefore, the seeds of the Cookzcreed Foundation were sown, with a vision to support aspiring chefs and address the challenges of the industry. However, just as our ideas were taking shape, tragedy struck, altering the course of my life forever.

MY STORY CONT.

The second week of January marked a profound loss in my life – the passing of Shaheed's mother. I remember the moment we found her in her room, a knot of dread forming in my stomach as I prayed it wasn't true. But as I stood there, time seemed to freeze, and the world became surreal, reminiscent of the day I lost my dear friend Sam. Witnessing death is a jolting experience; it grips you with a primal fear, rendering you breathless and disoriented. In those agonizing moments, as paramedics rushed in and the voices faded into a distant, I felt as though I were trapped in a nightmare, pleading with myself to wake up. The sound of mournful wails echoing from the room sunk into my bones, a haunting reminder of the raw anguish of loss. Yet, through that darkest moment, I've come to realize that death bestows upon us a profound gift – a stark reminder of our own mortality and the delicate beauty of life. It instills within us a deep appreciation for every fleeting moment and the precious souls that grace our journey.

But the pain didn't end there. Just a week later, Shaheed passed away, leaving behind a void that no words could fill. Despite my efforts to console and support him, his battle with mental illness ultimately claimed him. As I was confronted with the weight of grief and despair, little did I know that the challenges of 2020 were only beginning to unfold with the onset of the pandemic. With no distractions of work and competition, I found myself drowning in sorrow, overwhelmed with depression, guilt, and thoughts of suicide. Grief, I learned, is an unforgiving beast, lurking in the shadows of memories and striking when you least expect it. Yet, through the dark, there emerged a flicker of hope. With the support of therapy and the passage of time, I began to navigate the treacherous waters of grief, slowly finding peace in the routine of everyday life. It wasn't easy – there were days when the weight of the sadness threatened to consume me entirely, that I was drowning with no rescue in sight. But with each passing day, I found a glow of bravery within me, courage to stand tall and walk my way back to the light. Taking on a part-time role at a mental health center not only provided a sense of purpose but also served as a lifeline in my own journey towards healing. It took two and a half grueling years, marked by moments of anguish and fading glimpses of hope, but slowly, I began to find my footing once again. The journey of grief is ever lasting. You never really "get over it", you just learn to navigate it better each day without judgement.

In April 2020, I embarked on a journey that would not only shape the lives of others but also became an aid for my own healing. Establishing Cookzcreed Foundation was my way of honoring Shaheed's memory, but little did I realize the profound impact it would have on my own growth. What began as a humble endeavor to carry forward shared visions has blossomed into something far beyond my wildest dreams. Through partnerships with incredible organizations and individuals, doors have opened to opportunities I never dared imagine. In the process, I discovered facets of myself I never knew existed – a newfound sense of being and authenticity.

My journey through grief has taught me a valuable lesson – that it's okay to embrace the complexity of our emotions, to hold space for both joy and sorrow simultaneously. This wisdom, imparted by my grief therapist, has become the guiding principle of the Cookzcreed Foundation. We are not just a support system; we are a sanctuary, a safe haven where individuals can explore their own paths and find the solace they seek.

Stories are the threads that weave our lives together, offering a glance into the very essence of who we are and why we do what we do. By sharing my story with you, I hope to illuminate the path towards healing, resilience, and profound gratitude for every moment life offers us. Here's to the journey of self-discovery, to navigate our way through this life, and to cherishing every precious moment along the way.

FIND ME HERE...

https://canvasrebel.com/meet-kisha-washington/

https://www.coworkfrederick.com/member-spotlight-kisha-washington/

https://boldjourney.com/meet-kisha-washington/

https://worldfoodchampionships.com/talent/profile/our-competitors/6580/kisha-washington

https://chefswithoutrestaurants.com/2020/08/04/the-chefs-without-restaurants-podcast-episode-55-chef-kisha-washington-a-discussion-about-the-personal-chef-business-her-platform-for-chefs-and-a-culinary-non-profit/?amp

https://www.thekeyingredientllc.com/about

https://www.tiktok.com/@dyanmaine?_t=8l9RyrIWkE2&_r=1

https://chowco.org/2022/02/28/february-chow-corner/

https://tableathome.com/2018/04/best-private-chefs-washington-d-c-dmv/

https://theriver953.com/podcast/cookzcreed-2

foundation-/https://www.foodnetwork.com/shows/bakers-vs-fakers/episodes/brownie-points

https://www.jamesbeard.org/blog/2023-2024-legacy-network-cohort

UNDERSTANDING MENTAL HEALTH IN THE CULINARY WORLD

"IF I'M AN ADVOCATE FOR ANYTHING, IT'S TO MOVE. AS FAR AS YOU CAN, AS MUCH AS YOU CAN. ACROSS THE OCEAN, OR SIMPLY ACROSS THE RIVER. WALK IN SOMEONE ELSE'S SHOES OR AT LEAST EAT THEIR FOOD. IT'S A PLUS FOR EVERYBODY."– ANTHONY BOURDAIN

Quick culinary and hospitality statistics

- More than four out of every five hospitality workers reported increased stress levels.
- 45% of respondents stated they would not recommend working in the hospitality field
- 62% of respondents believed that the hospitality industry does not do enough for the physical and mental health of employees
- 74% of hospitality workers reported suffering verbal abuse from customers
- 24% of hospitality workers have required medical or psychological treatment for mental health issues
- Only one in every ten workers stated that they had access to mental health awareness training.
- More specifically, 38% of participants said they had dealt with depression, 49% suffered from sleeping disorders and a shocking 70% said that they'd experienced anxiety as a result of working in a restaurant.

Research on mental health issues

Most common Mental Health Challenges in the hospitality is, Depression and Burnout. Other challenges include Stress, Anxiety, Substance abuse, and Eating Disorders.

Stigma and Barriers

- Stigma- fear of judgement or discrimination
- Lack of awareness- not aware of the signs/resources
- Financial Barriers- cost of therapy or treatment
- Fear of job loss- jeopardizing their job security
- Lack of Support- support systems to seek help

www.datamyte.com

SUBSTANCE ABUSE IN THE CULINARY INDUSTRY

"RECOVERY IS A PROCESS. IT TAKES TIME. IT TAKES PATIENCE. IT TAKES EVERYTHING YOU'VE GOT."– UNKNOWN

Substance Abuse

- The Substance Abuse and Mental Health Services reports that the restaurant industry is the most at risk for illicit drug use and substance abuse disorders, with 17% of workers diagnosed with a substance abuse disorder.
SAMSA

Substance Abuse Break Down

- 1 in 10 Food service industry workers reported that they are under the influence of drugs for the majority of their shift, and 1 in 20 reported the same for Alcohol use.

Most used drugs:
- 81% Marijuana
- 31% Pain Killers
- 28% Cocaine

Alcohol Abuse

Most used Alcohol
- 61% Beer
- 47% Straight Liquor
- 37% Mixed Drink

Research

- 40% Consider casual substance use to be a part of their work culture.
Americanaddictioncenters.org

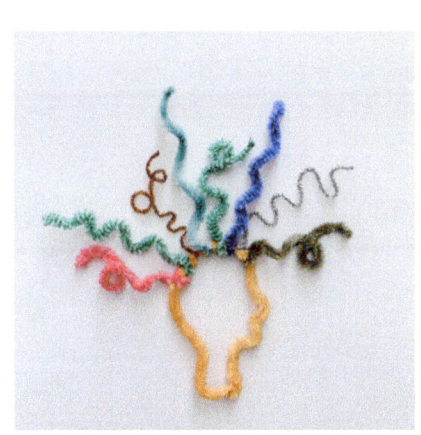

WWW.COOKZCREEDFOUNDATION.COM

MENTAL HEALTH STATISTICS

- "SLOW BREATHING IS LIKE AN ANCHOR IN THE MIDST OF AN EMOTIONAL STORM: THE ANCHOR WON'T MAKE THE STORM GO AWAY, BUT IT WILL HOLD YOU STEADY UNTIL IT PASSES." — *RUSS HARRIS*

THE SCOPE OF MENTAL HEALTH NATIONALLY

- More than 1 in 5 US adults live with Mental Illness. Over 1 in 5 youth (ages 13-18) either currently or at some point during their life, have has serious debilitating mental illness.
- About 1 in 25 US adult's live with a serious mental illness such as Schizophrenia, bipolar disorder, or major depression.
- Adults ages 35-44 also experienced the highest increase in mental health diagnoses, 45% reported a mental illness in 2023 compared with 31% in 2019- though adults ages 18-34 still reported the highest rate of mental illness at 50% in 2023.

Nami,
https://www.nami.org/mhstats

Key Findings

- In the US, there are 350 individuals for every 1 mental health provider.
- More than 2.7 million youth are experiencing severe major depression.
- 60% of youth with major depression do not receive mental health treatment.
- Over 12.1 million adults (4.8%) report serious thoughts of suicide.

2023
mhanational,org

SUBSTANCE ABUSE AT A GLANCE

"THERE IS NO SHAME IN BEGINNING AGAIN, FOR YOU GET A CHANCE TO BUILD BIGGER AND BETTER THAN BEFORE."
–AUTHOR UNKNOWN

Substance Abuse

- 50.0%, Half of people 12 and older have used illicit drugs at least once.
- Drug overdose deaths in the US since 2000 are nearing one (1) million.
- The federal budget for drug control in 2020 was $35 billion.

Alcohol Abuse

- 86.4% of people ages 18 or older report drinking alcohol at some point in their lifetime
- 70.1% report drinking in the past year
- 56% report drinking in the past month

Substance Abuse deaths

- Over 70,000 drug overdose deaths occur in the US annually.
- The number of overdose deaths increases at an annual rate of 4.0%

www.drugabusesatistics.org

Veteran Substance Abuse

- 7% of veterans struggle with illegal drug use compared to 5.3% of the general population in the US over age 18.
- 80% struggle with alcohol abuse, and 7% have an issue with both alcohol and illegal drugs.
- 7% of the veteran population has a serious mental illness compared to 14.4% of adults over 18.

ALABAMA-GEORGIA

"MENTAL HEALTH...IS NOT A DESTINATION, BUT A PROCESS. IT'S ABOUT HOW YOU DRIVE, NOT WHERE YOU'RE GOING." — *NOAM SHPANCER, PHD*

Alabama

Alabama Department of Mental Health
mh.alabama.gov
Elk River Treatment Program (Teen)
elkrivertreatment.com
Intergrated Behavioral Health
ibhvs.com

Alaska

Division of Behavioral Health
health.alaska.gov
Alaska Behavioral Health Association
alaskabha.org

Arizona

Arizona Health Care Cost Containment System
azahcccs.gov
Serenity Mental Health Centers
serenitymentalhealthcenters.com

Arkansas

Arkansas Department of Human Services
humanservices.arkansas.gov
Capstone
capstonetreatmentcenter.com (teen, young adult, men)

California

Mental Health Services Division
dhcs.ca.gov
Los Angeles Outpatient Center
laopcenter.com

Colorado

Colorado Department of Human Services
cdhs.colorado.gov
Mile High Behavioral Healthcare
milehighbehavioralhealthcare.org

ALABAMA-GEORGIA CONT...

Connecticut

Department of Mental Health and Addiction Services
portal.ct.gov/dmhas

Delaware

Division of Substance Abuse and Mental health
dhss.delaware.gov
Delaware Behavioral Health
delawarebehavioralhealth.org

Florida

Florida Mental Health
floridahealth.gov
The Sylvia Brafman Mental Health Center
slyviabrafman.com
Florida Oasis
thefloridaoasis.org

Georgia

Georgia Department of Behavioral Health and DD
dbhdd.georgia.gov
Balance Behavioral Health
balancebehavioral.health

Picture By Chef Terence Tomlin

Picture By Chef Kisha Washington

QUICK STATISTICS FOR MENTAL HEALTH IN THE STATES ALABAMA THROUGH GEORGIA

- In 2019, suicide was the twelfth leading cause of death in AL.
- In Alabama, 214,000 adults have a serious mental illness.
  site: alabamapublichealth.gov
  site: NAMI, Alabama

- Feb 2023, 32% of adults in Alaska reported symptoms of anxiety and depression.
  site: www.kff.org

- Arizona ranks 49 with a higher prevalence of mental illness and lower rates of access to care. www.namisa.org

- 27.5% of Arkansans reported symptoms associated with diagnoses of generalized anxiety disorder over that same period www.arkansasonline.com

- Nearly 1 in 7 California adults experiences a mental illness, and one in 26 has a serious mental illness that makes it difficult to carry out daily activities. www.chcf.org

- Colorado males are more than three times as likely to commit suicide as females.
- Colorado's suicide rate of 19.1 per 100,000 residents (2012) is the nation's sixth highest. www.coloradohealthinstitute.org

- In February 2021, 40.6% of adults in Connecticut reported symptoms of anxiety or depression. 22.3% were unable to get needed counseling or therapy. www.nami.org

- In Delaware the rate of drug overdose deaths has increased from 6.7 per 100,000 to 48.4 per 100,000 in 2019, which is a heavy increase www.myhealthycommunity.dhss.delaware

- Over 50 million Americans have a mental illness, but more than half 55% of adults with a mental illness don't receive treatment. www.floridatrend.com

- Just over 1.4 million Georgians suffer from at least one mental illness. This represents approximately 18% of the population.
- 314,000 adults have serious thoughts of suicide. www.newviewmh.com

HAWAII–MARYLAND

"JUST BECAUSE NO ONE ELSE CAN HEAL OR DO YOUR INNER WORK FOR YOU DOESN'T MEAN YOU CAN, SHOULD, OR NEED TO DO IT ALONE." – LISA OLIVERA

Hawaii

Adult Mental Health Division
health.hawaii.gov/amhd/
Pacific Quest
pacificquest.org

Idaho

Idaho Department of Health and Welfare
healthandwelfare.idaho.gov
Live Well Psychiatry
livewellpsychiatry.com

Indiana

Family and Social Service Administration
in.gov/fssa/dmha/home/
Indiana Council
indianacouncil.org

Iowa

Iowa Department of Health and Human Services
hhs.iowa.gov/mhds
Walnut Creek Psychiatry
walnutcreekpsych.com

Illinois

Illinois Department of Human Services
dhs.state.il.us
Next Level Counseling
nextlevelcounseling.org

Kansas

Kansas Behavioral Health Services
kdads.ks.gov
Soma Therapy and Psychiatric Services
somawitchita.com

Kentucky

Kentucky Cabinet of Health and Family Services
dbhdid.ky.gov/dbh
Crossroads
crossroadstreatmentcenters.com

HAWAII-MARYLAND CONT...

Louisana

Louisana Department of Health
ldh.la.gov
Lake Charles Memorial Health System
lcmh.com

Maine

Department of Health and Human Services
maine.gov/dhhs
Liberty Bay Recovery Center
libertybayrecovery.com

Maryland

Mental Health Association of MD
mhamd.org
Black Mental Health Alliance
blackmentalhealth.com
Brightwell Health
brightwellhealthcare.com

Picture by Chef Catina Smith

Picture by the late Chef Shaheed Claiborne

QUICK STATISTICS FOR MENTAL HEALTH IN THE STATES HAWAII THROUGH MARYLAND

- From February 1 to 13, 2023, 26.5% of adults in Hawaii reported symptoms of anxiety and/or depressive disorder, compared to 32.3% of adults in the U.S.

- In 2021, 20.1% of adolescents (ages 12-17) and 8.3% of adults in the U.S. reported having a major depressive episode in the past year.
www.kff.org

- Top 3 mental health issues in Idaho are: depression, anxiety, schizophrenia and mood or personality disorders,
www.kff.org

- The shortage of mental health providers is particularly dangerous for children, who are especially vulnerable to self-harm. The rate of youth suicides in Indiana is increasing due to poor access to care and other issues, according to IU Health officials.
www.indystar.com

- Drug overdose death rates have increased in Illinois from 10.9 per 100,000 in 2011 to 29 per 100,000 in 2021.
www,kff,org

- Nearly 41,000 adults have serious thoughts of suicide. 14,000 adults made a suicide plan, and 5,000 adults attempted suicide in Indiana.
www.fsph.iupui.edu

- In February 2021, 42.2% of adults in Iowa experienced anxiety and depression with 25.4% not getting the needed treatment or therapy.
www.bja.ojp.gov

- In 2022 annual report, Kansas ranked 51st in the country. Last in the category of youth with substance use disorder, and 48th out of 51 in adults with a mental illness and adults with serious thoughts of suicide. 48th in the category of access to care.
www.kmuw.org

- Suicide is the second leading cause of death for youth and young adults in Kentucky.
www.education.ky.gov

- In 2021, there were 1,335 opioid overdose deaths in Louisiana, which accounted for 54% of all drug overdose deaths in the state.
www.kff.org

- In Maine, 61,000 adults have a serious mental illness, and 14,000 teen Mainers age 12-17 have depression.
www.namimaine.org

- In 2021, 20.1 % of adolescents and 8.3% of adults in the US reported having a major depressive episode in the past year in Maryland.

MASSACHUSETTS-NEW JERSEY

"I'M NOT TELLING YOU IT IS GOING TO BE EASY. I'M TELLING YOU IT'S GOING TO BE WORTH IT!" – ANONYMOUS

Massachusetts

Massachusetts Department of Mental Health
mass.gov/orgs/massachusetts-department-of-mental-health
Aspire Health Alliance
aspirehealthalliance.org

Michigan

Community Mental Health Services
michigan.gov/mdhhs
Hope Network
hopenetwork.org

Minnesota

Department of Human Services
mn.gov/dhs/dhs.state.mn.us
Lakeland Mental Health Center
lmhc.org

Mississippi

Mississippi Department of Mental Health
dmh.ms.gov
North Mississippi State Hospital
nmsh.state.ms.us

MASSACHUSETTS- NEW JERSEY CONT...

Missouri

Missouri Department of Mental Health
dmh.mo.gov/behavioral-health
Comtrea Health Center
comtrea.org

Montana

Montana Department Human Health Services
dphhs.mt.gov
Cedar Creek Integrated Health
cedarcreekintergratedhealth.org

Nebraska

Nebraska Department of Health and Human Services
dhhs.ne.gov
Center Pointe
centerpointe.org

Nevada

Behavioral Health Services
dhcfp.nv.gov
Nevada Mental Health
nevadamentalhealth.com

New Hampshire

New Hampshire Department of Health and Human Services
dhhs.nh.gov
Center State Wellness
centerstatewellness.com

New Jersey

Department of Human Services
state.nj.us/humanservices
Harmony Bay Wellness
harmonybaywellness.com

Picture By Chef Kisha

QUICK STATISTICS FOR MENTAL HEALTH IN THE STATES MASSACHUSETTS THROUGH NEW JERSEY

- Around 36% of Massachusetts youth ages 0-17 experienced at least one form of trauma, abuse, or significant stress in the prior year, with almost 14% experiencing multiple trauma.
www.mamh.org

- In 2020, 268,000 Massachusetts residents thought about suicide, while 740 died of it.
www.arkbh.com

- In Michigan, 15% of adults had substance use disorder if which 93.5% did not receive treatment.

- 11% of adults in Michigan with mental illness are uninsured.
www.brightpinepsychology.com

- About 5.7% of Minnesota adults needed treatment for alcohol use disorders and about 2.1% needed treatment for drug use disorder.
www.leg.mn.gov

- Mississippi ranks 10th out of 50 for 158,000 adults with a substance abuse disorder in the past year, 19th out of 50 with 20.16% of adults with any mental illness, 41st out of 50 with 118,000 adults with thoughts of suicide, and 47th out of 50, for access to care.
www.viksburgnews.com

- In Missouri, 39% of adults reported symptoms of anxiety and depression. 28% were unable to get needed counseling or therapy.
www.namimissouri.org

- Montana is number 1 in the nation for suicides. An estimated 64,000 Montanans have a substance use disorder. There has been a 427% increase in meth violations from 2011-2015. 90% of Montanans with SUD are not receiving treatment.
www.montanabehavioralhealth.org

- Nearly 1 and 5 Nebraskans has a diagnosable mental health or substance use disorder.
www.journalstar.com

- 38.4% of adults in Nevada reported symptoms of anxiety and or depression disorder, compared to 32.3% of adults in the whole US. In 2021, there was 605 opioid overdose deaths in Nevada.

- In New Hampshire, 44% of youth felt sad or hopeless almost every day for two weeks or more. Nearly 10% of youth in NH attempted suicide at least once.
www.extension.unh.edu

- In New Jersey, 248,000 adults have a serious mental illness.
www.nami.org

OUR INTERACTIVE SURVEY

What are chefs saying about the kitchen? *Note, all answers are anonymous

Question Asked:
What Has Been Your Expereince Working In Multiple Kitchens?

-"My experiernce has been ok. A lot of kitchens are run strict, some not so much, I like structure"

Question Asked:
What Do You Think Of The Chef System In The Kitchen? Has It Served You?

"The chef sysytem has served served me well."

"I feel that it has, but trying to move up the ranks has been tough"

Question Asked:
Do You Believe Chefs Get Paid What They Are Worth?

"Absoultely not. We are worth a lot and people dont get that"

"Some clients don't understand what goes into making a meal, its a lot, to get paid so little."

Question Asked:
Has Culinary School Served You? Or Has Being In The Kitchen Learning Been Better For You?

"School has served me, but I learned a lot on my own."

"Hands on experience in the kitchen serves well, I would recommend to any new chef."

Question Asked:
What Would Be Your Ideal Work Schedule? What Should Restaurant Owners Offer Employees?

_Not ideal but my evenings or weekends back."

"As a private chef, 3 hish end dinners a month"

Question Asked:
What Area Of Culinary Or Hospitality Needs To Be Talked About More, or Shed Light On?

"Inclusion, funding, women in the kitchen, drinking or alcohol as an award."

WWW.COOKZCREEDFOUNDATION.COM

NEW MEXICO-SOUTH CAROLINA

"START LISTENING TO THE WAY YOU TALK TO YOURSELF. THESE INTERACTIONS WILL TELL YOU HOW WELL YOU KNOW YOURSELF, HOW MUCH YOU RESPECT YOURSELF, AND WHAT BOUNDARIES YOU ARE LACKING." — SARA KUBURIC

New Mexico

New Mexico Health
nmhealth.org
La Casa Behavioral Health
lacasahealth.com

New York

New York State Office of Mental Health
omh.ny.gov
Mental Health Association in NY
mhanys.org

North Carolina

Adult Mental Health Services
ncdhhs.gov
Mental Health Association
triadmentalhealth.org

North Dakota

North Dakota Health and Human Services
hhs.nd.gov
Inspired Life Wellness Center
inspired-lifewellness.com

Ohio

Ohio Mental Health Addiction Services
mha.ohio.gov
Ohio Health Outpatient Behavioral Health
ohiohealth.com

Picture By Chef Keema

NEW MEXICO-SOUTH CAROLINA CONT...

Oklahoma

Oklahoma Mental Health and Substance Abuse
oklahoma.gov/odmhsas
Red Rock Behavioral Health
red-rock.com

Oregon

Oregon Behavioral Health Services
oregon.gov
Crisis Assessment and Treatment Center
www.telecorp.com/multnomah-catc

Pennsylvania

Department of Human Services
dhs.pa.gov
Pennsylvania Behavioral Health Center
pennsylvaniabehavioralhealth.com

Rhode Island

Community Mental Health Center
bhddh.ri.gov
Life Span
lifespan.org

South Carolina

South Carolina Department of Mental Health
scdmh.net
Prisma Behavioral Health
prismahealth.org

QUICK STATISTICS FOR MENTAL HEALTH IN THE STATES NEW MEXICO THROUGH SOUTH CAROLINA

- Suicide is the 2nd leading cause of death for New Mexico residents 15 to 44.

- 533 suicide deaths or about 10 per week on average.
  www.nmhealth.org

- 1 in 2 (50.7%) New Yorkers who lost employment income since the onset of the pandemic reported anxiety and/or depression.

- 8% of NYC public high school students report attempting suicide.
  www.nyhealthfoundation.org
  www.nyc.gov

- North Carolina rates of anxiety and depression quadrupled 2019-2021 11%-41%

- Drug overdose deaths jumped 72% in two years.
  www.ncdhhs.gov

- Between 1999-2016, suicide rose by 58% in North Dakota.

- In 2020, 19.2% of North Dakota residents had been diagnosed with some form of depression.
  www.shiftnursing.com

- In Ohio, 478,000 adults have a serious mental illness. In 2021, 1838 lives were lost to suicide.
  www.nami.org

- Oklahoma ranks 5th (25.6%) in the nation for rates of Any Mental Illness.

- 35.3% of adults in Oregon reported symptoms of anxiety and/or depression disorder, compared to the 32.3% in the U.S.
  www.kff.org

- Pennsylvania ranks 17th nationally with 51.9% of adults suffering from mental illness (more than 1 million) people untreated.
  www.haponline.org

- 178,000 adults in Rhode Island have a mental health condition. 9000 Rhode Islanders age 12-17 have depression.
  www.nami.org

- South Carolina ranks 35th in the nation for prevalence of mental illness in adults, and 48th in the nation for prevalence of mental illness in children.
  www.charlestoncitypaper.com

Picture by Chef Kisha

SOUTH DAKOTA-WYOMING

"MY DARK DAYS MADE ME STRONGER. OR MAYBE I ALREADY WAS STRONG, AND THEY MADE ME PROVE IT." — EMERY LORD

South Dakota

South Dakota Department Social Services
dss.sd.gov
Sioux River Mental Health Services
siouxrivermentalhealth.com

Tennessee

Department of Mental Health and Substance Abuse Services
tn.gov/behavioral-health
Arbor Wellness
arborwellnessmh.com

Texas

Texas Health and Human Services
hhs.texas.gov
Forefront Behavioral Health
fbhaustin.com

Utah

Wasatch Behavioral Health
wasatch.org
Embark Behavioral Health
embarkbh.com

Vermont

Department of Mental Health
mentalhealth.vermont.gov
Vermont Family Network
vermontfamilynetwork.org

SOUTH DAKOTA- WYOMING CONT...

Virginia

Virginia Department of Behavioral Health
dbhds.virginia.gov
Bloom Health Centers
bloomhealthcenters.com/winchester-va/

Washington (State)

Washington State Department of Social and Health Services
dshs.wa.gov
The Center place of Hope
aplaceofhope.com

Washington D.C

Department of Behavioral Health
dbh.dc.gov
United Way of NCA
unitedwaynca.org

West Virginia

Bureau of Behavioral Health
dhhr.wv.gov
Renovo Center
renovocenter.com

Wisconsin

Wisconsin Department of Health
dhs.wisconsin.gov
Journey Mental Health Center
journeymhc.org

Wyoming

Wyoming Department of Health
health.wyo.gov
Cody Regional Health
codyregionalhealth.org

Picture By Chef Liktha Gali

QUICK STATISTICS FOR MENTAL HEALTH IN THE STATES SOUTH DAKOTA THROUGH WYOMING

- In 2021, 198 South Dakotans died by suicide. This is higher than in 2019 and 2020, which each had 185 suicides, and is highest ever recorded in the state.
www.resilienttoday.org

- In Tennessee, 1 in 5 children have a mental health disorder and 1 in 20 teens has a substance abuse disorder, and a large percentage of children and adolescents with behavioral health challenges do not receive care.
www.memphis.edu

- Of more than 7 million Texans ages 17 and younger, more than 1.2 million report a mental, emotional, behavioral, or developmental problem. That's 20% of all Texas youth.
www.evertexan.org

- In Utah, 139,000 adults have serious mental illness. 51,000 Utahans aged 12-17 have depression.
www.abc4.com

- 1 in 6 in Vermont adults report poor mental health, with disparities reported among younger adults 26%. 6% of Vermont adults have seriously considered suicide.
www.healthvermont.gov

- 1,115,000 adults in Virginia have a mental health condition. 97,000 Virginians ages 12-17 have depression.
www.nami.org

- 1 in 20 Washington (State) adults report serious thoughts of suicide. Nearly 1 in 4 Washington adults with mental illness report an unmet need for treatment.
www.seattletimes.com

- In February 2021, 43.7% of adults in Washington DC reported symptoms of anxiety or depression.
www.nami.org

- 27.5% of West Virginians reported being diagnosed with depression.
www..wvpublic.org

- Drug overdose death rates have increased in West Virginia from 36.3 per 100,000 in 2011 to 90.9 per 100,000 in 2021.
www.kff.org

- Nearly 5% of Wisconsin residents, or 219,000 people, have reported serious thoughts of suicide, which is slightly higher than the national percentage.
www.greenbaypressgazette.com

- 88,000 adults in Wyoming have a mental health condition. 612 people in Wyoming are homeless and 1 in 8 live with a serious mental illness.

SITE SPECIFIC: WASHINGTON D.C., MARYLAND, NORTHERN VA

"WE WANT YOU TO KNOW THAT YOU DON'T NEED TO BE IN CRISIS OR DISTRESS TO SEEK HELP AS GOING TO THERAPY HAS NUMEROUS BENEFITS." – CARLA AVALOS LCSW+PMH-C

Resources for Washington, DC

NAMI Washington DC- providing education, support and advocacy for families and individuals.
www.namidc.org
Helpline: 202-466-0972

Active Minds- nonprofit organization promoting mental health awareness and education for young adults.
www.activeminds.org

Resources for Maryland

Covenant Psychiatric and Mental Health Services
www.covenant-cares.org

Passionate Behavioral Health Center
www.pbhcinc.com

Resources for Virginia

AMFM Mental Health Treatment Center- for mood and thought disorders
www.amfmtreatment.com

Bloom Health Centers- multiple locations throughout the DMV area.
www.bloomhealthcenters.com

Embark Behavioral Health
www.embarkbh.com

Winchester Community Mental Health Center
www.winchestercmhc.org

WEBSITES/LINKS

"VULNERABILITY SOUNDS LIKE TRUTH AND FEELS LIKE COURAGE. TRUTH AND COURAGE AREN'T ALWAYS COMFORTABLE, BUT THEY'RE NEVER WEAKNESS." — BRENÉ BROWN

Resources for Suicidal Ideations, Depression, and Anxiety

Nami
www.nami.org
The Trevor Project
www.thetrevorproject.org
Zero Suicide Alliance
www.zerosuicealliance.com
To Write Love on Her Arms
www.twloha.com
The Depression Project
www.thedepressionproject.com
Breaking Taboo
www.breaking-taboo.org
Suicidology
www.suicidology.org
American Foundation of Suicide Prevention
www.afsp.org
How Mental
www.howmental.com

Resources for Men

Heads Up Guys
www.headsupguys.org
Man Therapy
www.mantherapy.org

Resources for Teens and Adolecents

16 Strong Project
www.16strongproject.com
Teens 4 Teens Help
www.teens4teenshelp.org

Resources for LGBTQ+

Pride Institute
www.pride-institute.com
PFLAG
www.pflag.org
It Gets Better Project
www.itgetsbetter.org
LGBT National Youth Hotline
Call 800-246-7743
LGBT National Hotline
Call 888-843-4564

Resources Hispanic/Latin/Asian/Native American/Pacific Islander

National Alliance of Hispanic Health
https://www.healthyamericas.org/
Asian and Pacific Islander American Health Forum
https://www.apiahf.org/

MEN WEBSITES/LINKS

"I'M A MAN, AND NO LESS OF A MAN FOR ADMITTING 'I'M NOT OKAY,' AND FOR OPENLY TALKING ABOUT THE CONSTANT STRUGGLE AND BATTLE I FACE WITH MYSELF EVERY SINGLE DAY." —JOE PLUMB.

Men Mental Health Statistics

5 Leading Health Issues for Men
Depression- 6 million men suffer from depression each year
Panic and Anxiety- 3 million have panic disorder or phobia
Bipolar Disorder- 1 million men develop BP disorder between 16-25
Schizophrenia- out of all people diagnosed, age 30, around 90% are men
Eating Disorder- 10% of people with anorexia or bulimia are men
www.goodrxhealth.com

Resources

Men's Group
www.mensgroup.com
The Men's List
www.themenslist.com
CHOW all mens meeting
https://chowco.org/events/chow-wednesday-mens-meeting-virtual-2023/
Black Men Heal
https://blackmenheal.org/
Therapy for Black Men
https://therapyforblackmen.org/

WOMEN WEBSITES/LINKS

""IT'S OKAY IF YOU FALL DOWN AND LOSE YOUR SPARK. JUST MAKE SURE THAT WHEN YOU GET BACK UP, YOU RISE AS THE WHOLE DAMN FIRE." – COLETTE WERDEN

Women Mental Health Statistics

Each year 1 and 5 women in the U.S has a mental health problem such as depression, PTSD, or eating disorder

Women are twice as likely to be diagnosed with anxiety as men

www.womenshealth.gov

Resources

Safe Project
www.safeproject.us
Society of Women's Health Research
https://swhr.org/
Black Mental Wellness
https://www.blackmentalwellness.com/
Therapy for Black Girls
https://www.therapyforblackgirls.com
Kinder in the Keys Treatment Center
https://kinderinthekeys.com/

CHEF WEBSITES FOR TOOLS AND ITEMS

"JUST ONE SMALL POSITIVE THOUGHT IN THE MORNING CAN CHANGE YOUR WHOLE DAY." —DALAI LAMA

Chefs Clothing (Jackets, Aprons, etc.)

Tilit
tilitnyc.com

Chef Works
chefworks.com

Chef Uniforms
chefuniforms.com

Chef Toys
cheftoys.com

Boldric
boldric.com

Chef Equipment (Dishware, Knives, etc.)

Fortessa Store (Local)
fortessa.com

Williams Sonoma
williams-sonoma.com

APPS

"BE THE CHANGE THAT YOU WISH TO SEE IN THE WORLD." – MAHATMA GANDHI

APPS: Downloadable via Android and Apple

BetterHelp
- Therapy Platform
- Prices: $60-$90 per week

Calm
- Designed to help manage stress, sleep, and live better
- Subscription service

Headspace
- Meditation and Mindfulness tools
- Plan based platform

Talkspace
- Therapy Platform
- Subscription plans available

BOOKS, PODCAST, SERIES

"PODCASTING ALLOWS ME TO HAVE A CONVERSATION WITH MY AUDIENCE IN A WAY THAT FEELS MORE PERSONAL AND INTIMATE." – <u>REBECCA WATSON, HOST OF THE SKEPCHICK PODCAST</u>

Books for Mental Health

Willow Weep for Me (For Black Women with depression)
The Power of Now, by Eckhart Tolle
The Secret To Unlock The Stress Life (Burnout)
Boundaries
Self Compassion

TV Series

The Final Table (Netflix)
Pressure Cooker (Netflix)
Iron Chef (Netflix)
Five Star Kitchen (Netflix)
School of Chocolate (Netflix)
Top Chef (Bravo)
Tournament Of Champions (Food Network)
24 in 24 (Food Network)

Podcast

Chefs Without Restaurants
www.chefswithoutrestaurants.com
Chef PSA
www.chefspsa.com

HELP LINES/CRISIS LINES

"IN EVERY CRISIS, DOUBT OR CONFUSION, TAKE THE HIGHER PATH – THE PATH OF COMPASSION, COURAGE, UNDERSTANDING AND LOVE." AMIT RAY

Crisis Hotlines

National Suicide Prevention Hotline
Dial 988 (US Only)
Call 800-273-8255
Call 888-628-9454 (Spanish)

Crisis Text Line
Text "HOME" to 741741
www.crisistextline.org

Self Injury Hotline
Call 800-366-8288

SAMHSA National Helpline
Call 800-662-4357

Rehab Assistance
Call 866-658-3750

CULINARY/HOSPITALITY SPECIFIC ORGANIZATIONS

"COLLABORATION IS A KEY PART OF THE SUCCESS OF ANY ORGANIZATION, EXECUTED THROUGH A CLEARLY DEFINED VISION AND MISSION AND BASED ON TRANSPARENCY AND CONSTANT COMMUNICATION."-DINESH PALIWAL

Organizations

The * are organizations that have contributed

Healthy Pour
https://healthypour.org/
Restaurant After Hours*
https://www.restaurantafterhours.org/
CHOW*
www.chowco.org
James Beard Foundation
www.jamesbeard.org
Cooks Who Care*
@cookswhocare
Not 9 to 5*
www.not9to5.org
Ben's Friends
www.bensfriendshope.com
Heard
@heard_org
The Burnt Chef project
theburntchefproject.com

CULINARY/HOSPITALITY FOR HIGH SCHOOL AND COLLEGE STUDENTS

"DREAM BIG AND DARE TO FAIL." — NORMAN VAUGHAN

High School and College Programs /Schools

Whether you choose to go to culinary school or decide to stage in a kitchen, both are worth it in the culinary world.

Prostart
www.chooserestaurants.org/programs/prostart/

Escoffier School of Culinary Arts
www.escoffier.edu/

The Culinary Institute of America
www.ciachef.edu/

Johnson and Wales University
www.jwu.edu

Cooking Classes

Cookology
www.cookologyonline.com/

Sur La Table
www.surlatable.com

SPECIFIC TO CULINARY/HOSPITALITY VETERANS

"AFTER A TRAUMATIC EXPERIENCE, THE HUMAN SYSTEM OF SELF-PRESERVATION SEEMS TO GO ONTO PERMANENT ALERT, AS IF THE DANGER MIGHT RETURN AT ANY MOMENT." — JUDITH LEWIS HERMAN

Veterans

Veterans Crisis Line
Call 800-273-8255
Text 838255

Military One Source
www.militaryonesource.mil

The Wounded Warrior Project
www.woundedwarriorproject.org

Military Mental Health Statistics

From 2016-2020, a total of 456,293 active component service members were diagnosed with at least 1 mental health disorder.
www.health.mil

Research indicates that 14%-16% of the US service members deployed to Afghanistan and Iraq have been affected by PTSD or depression.
www.pubmed.ncbi.nlm.nih.gov

Veterans comprise 20% of suicides nationally and reports that 3 out of 5 veterans who died by suicide were diagnosed as having a mental health condition.
www.militarytimes.com

SPECIFIC TO CULINARY COMPETITION CHEFS AND HIGH PRESSURE FINE DINING

"CHAMPIONS DO NOT BECOME CHAMPIONS WHEN THEY WIN THE EVENT, BUT IN THE HOURS, WEEKS, MONTHS AND YEARS THEY SPEND PREPARING FOR IT. THE VICTORIOUS PERFORMANCE ITSELF IS MERELY THE DEMONSTRATION OF THEIR CHAMPIONSHIP CHARACTER." - T ALAN ARMSTRONG

Competition Cooking

Competition cooking or competitive cooking is something few chefs tackle. Its a different mindset but same application and skill set, then being in a regular kitchen. You have to think on the fly, pivot at every corner, and think ahead in the moment. It takes skill, a sense of urgency, and full creative energy to be fully present in competition. But, the ramifications of losing, and placing, or the adrenaline of the competition itself, can take a toll on your mind, body, and confidence. Especially anyone that has competed on TV, or large competitions. You are always trying to stay up to date on trends, constantly practicing, or trying new ingredients. It can sometimes be a whole other practice besides your chef job.

Michelin Restaurants/High Pressure Kitchens

For chefs working in Michelin Restaurants, this can be a whole other level of stress. Michelin Guide has started telling chefs when they're about to lose a star. Demotion of this magnitude causes strife, tears, loss of confidence, chef's reputations, hurt business and more. Two Michelin starred chefs have died by suicide in the past: Bernard Loiseau in 2003 and Benoit Violier in 2016.

www.robbreport.com

Some well know 3 michellin star restaurants include:
The Inn at Little Washington ***
Le Bernadin ***
Eleven Madison Park ***
Alinea ***
The French Laundry ***

Picture By Chef Jonathan Hicks

LET'S TALK ABOUT IT...

In my research and discussions with chefs and industry experts, one striking revelation is the delicate balance between constructive criticism and outright criticism, between valuable feedback and detrimental comments, and between positive reinforcement and hindering remarks. What outsiders might not fully grasp is the weight of negative feedback that chefs and hospitality professionals often bear, whether it's from customers, clients, employees, or employers. These critiques can deeply affect our confidence and self-perception as chefs, despite our dedication to our craft, our creativity, and our ability to thrive under pressure. It's important for those outside the industry to understand the emotional toll that constant scrutiny can take on chefs and hospitality workers.

When I spoke with several chefs, many shared experiences of being yelled at, belittled, or even physically harmed in the kitchen. While some aspects of kitchen culture have evolved, the mistreatment has shifted from physical to emotional and psychological abuse. Employers, supervisors, and colleagues can undermine your confidence, make your job unbearable, or even sabotage your career advancement. It's evident that the environment can turn toxic, but where did the spirit of collaboration, support, and mentorship go? Why does seeking help or trying to work together feel like an uphill battle? It's disheartening that instead of camaraderie, there's often a sense of competition and cruelty. While not every person is a good fit for everyone, there's a fine line between healthy competition and outright cruelty when you're constantly subjected to demeaning comments or actions from fellow chefs.

When it comes to those of us in the culinary and hospitality world, there's a lot we carry on our shoulders. We all began our journey from somewhere humble, so let's approach each other with kindness, tempered with honesty. Remember, there's strength in unity. Your fellow chef might just have that fresh perspective you've been searching for, or they could offer the support you desperately need. And above all, let's not forget the invisible battles we all face in our mental health. How would you want to be treated if you were in their shoes? A little compassion can go a long way in this demanding industry.

ENCOURAGING HEALTHY WORK ENVIORNMMENTS

"A POSITIVE WORK ENVIRONMENT IS THE FOUNDATION FOR PRODUCTIVITY AND EMPLOYEE WELL-BEING."
— DAX BAMANIA

Creating Healthy Work Environments

Training and Education with employees to reduce stigma.

Open communication for dialogue, and voicing concerns, team meetings, etc.

Implementing Health Policies such as employee assistance or counseling services.

Encouraging work and life balances with flexible scheduling, paid time off or vacations
www.datamyte.com

Essential Strategies

Hold regular meetings for updates and collaboration.

Investing in employee development, mentoring or coaching.

Zero tolerance for discrimination, harassment, Increase diversity and inclusion.

Recognition programs, milestones, peer to peer.
www.linkedin.com

SELF-CARE SIMPLE TECHNIQUES

"LIGHTEN UP ON YOURSELF. NO ONE IS PERFECT. GENTLY ACCEPT YOUR HUMANNESS." —DEBORAH DAY

Simple Self Care Techniques

Get Regular Exercise
Eat Healthy, Stay Hydrated
Sleep well
Relaxing Activities
Set Goals
Practice Gratitude
Stay Connected
www.nimh.nih.gov

Activities for Self Care

Meditation: Beginners: Sit for a few minutes, focus your breath, follow the breath for two minutes
www.mindful.org
Journaling: Reflective or Gratitude
www.dayoneapp.com
Nature Walk
Practice Mindfulness
Simple Practice:
Engaging all senses
Name 5 things you can see
Name 4 things you can touch
Name 3 things you can hear
Name 2 things you can smell
Name 1 thing you can taste
Breathing Exercise
Simple Practice:
4/4/4
Inhale for 4, Hold for 4, Exhale for 4

CONCLUSION

"THE QUALITY OF YOUR LIFE WILL BE DETERMINED BY THE QUALITY OF YOUR CONTRIBUTION. WHEN YOU WORK TO IMPROVE THE LIVES OF OTHERS, YOUR LIFE IMPROVES AUTOMATICALLY." – KUREK ASHLEY

I would like to thank all those that have contributed to this book, all the chefs for their work and stories, my friends and family, and my culinary/ hospitality /mental health friends. I do this work because I wish when I was a young cook and chef, that someone gave me the tools to build an easier path. So here is a tool, a steppingstone to building yours.

We are in the works for Volume 2 and Volume 3 of this three-part series. Here is a sneak peak of the next volume:

Volume 2: Elevating Mental Health Mindfulness and A Deeper Dive Into Navigating Chef/Hospitality Challenges.
Stay Tuned!!!

WWW.COOKZCREEDFOUNDATION.ORG

CONTRIBUTOR PAGES

CONTRIBUTOR OVERVIEW

"IT IS AN ABSOLUTE HUMAN CERTAINTY THAT NO ONE CAN KNOW HIS OWN BEAUTY OR PERCEIVE A SENSE OF HIS OWN WORTH UNTIL IT HAS BEEN REFLECTED BACK TO HIM IN THE MIRROR OF ANOTHER LOVING, CARING HUMAN BEING."
JOHN JOSEPH POWELL, <u>THE SECRET OF STAYING IN LOVE</u>

In the collaborative effort of crafting a culinary masterpiece, our Psychiatric Nurse Practioner brings their expertise, background and compassion ensuring every detail is tended to with care. Following are organizations dedicated to promoting health and wellness lending their knowledge, and advocating for sustainable practices. With their guidance, chefs, hospitality individuals, restaurateurs, cooks, bartenders, etc. learn to connect self-care with nutrition and skills set, fostering a deeper understanding of the interconnectedness between food and well-being. Lastly, seasoned chefs impart their wisdom, elevating dishes with innovative techniques and exquisite flavors, while mentoring aspiring cooks in the craft or creativity. Together, these diverse contributors bring a collective of experience, each one evolving and growing in their respective roles, ultimately creating a culinary tapestry that celebrates the intersection of health, community, and culinary artistry.

WWW.COOKZCREEDFOUNDATION.COM

Rebecca Myers-Settle
RN, MS, CMSRN, PMHNP-BC, NE-BC, CTTS

Rebecca Myers-Settle MSN, RN, NE-BC, PMHNP-BC, CTTS is a board-certified Nurse Executive and Psychiatric Nurse Practitioner. She is the owner of Blue Ridge Mental Healthcare, LLC in Front Royal, Virginia, Adjunct Nurse Faculty at Shenandoah University, president of the Virginia Chapter of the American Psychiatric Nurses Association, and member of the Lord Fairfax EMS Critical Incident Stress Management Team. Rebecca is an advocate of mental health and encourages individuals to never give up, practice self-care, and keep pushing forward through the challenges that might be facing them today because they are building a better tomorrow.

CONTACT INFORMATION:

Blue Ridge Mental Healthcare, LLC
Located at 624 Virginia Avenue
Front Royal, VA 22630
540-749-0579

The restaurant, food and beverage, and hospitality industries are known to be competitive, chaotic, stressful, perfectionistic, and overwhelming to those individuals working and navigating these fields. Workers often report experiencing bullying, being held to high standards and demands, working long hours, and earning lower wages. The incidents of substance misuse, burn-out, depression, anxiety, emotional exhaustion, and mental anguish have significantly increased amongst chefs, restaurant workers, and individuals employed in hospitality roles since 2020 and continues to rise. Resiliency is a key foundation for maintaining longevity and recovering from stressors. Recognizing when you are not in your best headspace and not ignoring the signs is extremely important.

Tips For Success

- Destigmatize mental health by seeking mental healthcare and encouraging others to do the same.
- Increase support to your team and peers and encourage healthy self-care rituals.
- Educate yourself and your team on signs and symptoms of psychological stress and act fast when identified.
- Create a healthy and effective peer support system. Partner with a peer and check-in routinely to discuss how each of you are feeling and how things are going. You can problem solve together.

Resources

988-National Suicide and Crisis Hotline
USBG National Charity Foundation
https://www.usbgfoundation.org/single-post/2018/06/25/resources-for-maintaining-your-mental-health-in-the-hospitality-industry
The Burnt Chef Project
https://www.theburntchefproject.com/learnmore/about

Blue Ridge Mental Healthcare, LLC

Today is your opportunity to build the tomorrow you want

Our Services:

- Personalized Mental Healthcare and Medication Management
- Mental Health Education & Psychotherapy
- ADHD Assessments and Treatment
- Substance Abuse & Addiction Management

Why Choose Us

Blue Ridge Mental Healthcare strives to meet your mental health needs through enhancing access to care and decreasing the stigma around mental health.

Accepting patients ages 5 years and older.

Accepting private pay, Medicare, Medicaid, and most major insurance carriers. Reach out today to learn how Blue Ridge Mental Healthcare can help you.

Contact Us:

- 540-749-0579
- www.blueridgementalhealthcare.com
- 624 Virginia Avenue
  Front Royal, VA 22630

International Critical Incident Stress Foundation, Inc.

Suicide Awareness and Prevention Resources

American Association of Suicidology www.suicidology.org	**Samaritans USA** www.samaritansusa.org
American Foundation for Suicide Prevention www.afsp.org	**Substance Abuse and Suicide Prevention: Evidence and Implications** **Center for Substance Abuse Treatment (CSAT), SAMHSA, HHS** www.samhsa.gov/matrix2/508SuicidePreventionPaperFinal.pdf
Charting the future of Suicide Prevention: A 2010 Progress Review of the National Strategy and Recommendations for the Decade Ahead, 2010 **Education Development Center, Inc.** www.sprc.org/library/ChartingTheFuture_Fullbook.pdf	**Suicide Awareness Voices of Education (SAVE)** www.save.org
International Association for Suicide Prevention (IASP) www. iasp.info	**Suicide Prevention Resource Center (SPRC) Best Practices Registry for Suicide Prevention** www.sprc.org/bpr
Mental Health America www.mentalhealthamerica.net	**The Trevor Project** www.thetrevorproject.org
National Council for Suicide Prevention (NCSP) www.ncsponline.org	**U.S. Department of Defense Suicide Prevention Website** www.health.mil/News_And_Multimedia/Special_Features/suicide-prevention-awareness.aspx
National Institute of Mental Health, NIH, HHS www.nimh.nih.gov	**U.S. Department of Defense/U.S. Department of Veterans Affairs Suicide Outreach** www.suicideoutreach.org
National Strategy for Suicide Prevention **National Action Alliance for Suicide Prevention** www.surgeongeneral.gov/library/reports/national-strategy-suicide-prevention/index.html	**U.S. Department of Veterans Affairs Suicide Prevention Website** www. veteranscrisisline.net
National Suicide Prevention Lifeline www.suicidepreventionlifeline.org	

3290 Pine Orchard Ln., Suite 106, Ellicott City, MD 21042 | 410-750-9600   ICISF.org

Permission for use by the International Critical Incident Stress Foundation.

NAMI NEVADA

MISSION

The mission of NAMI Northern Nevada is to advocate for a life of quality and dignity by providing education, resources and emotional support to families and those affected by mental illness. We strive to end discrimination and stigma for all persons affected by these illnesses through broader education and collaboration with the whole community. NAMI envisions a world where all people affected by mental illness live healthy, fulfilling lives supported by a community that cares.

Services

Family Support Group
https://naminorthernnevada.org/support-and-education/support-groups/nami-family-support-group/
Connections Recovery Group
https://naminorthernnevada.org/support-and-education/support-groups/nami-connection/
Family to Family Educational Course
https://naminorthernnevada.org/support-and-education/mental-health-education/nami-family-to-family/
Peer to Peer Educational Course
https://naminorthernnevada.org/support-and-education/mental-health-education/nami-peer-to-peer/

Resources

Nevada Warmline (Crisis Support)
https://namiwesternnevada.org/resources/nevada-warmline/
Nevada Teen Text Line
https://namiwesternnevada.org/resources/nevada-teen-peer-support-text-line/
Nevada Caring Contacts
https://namiwesternnevada.org/resources/nevada-caring-contacts/

CONTACT INFORMATION:

info@naminorthernnevada.org
www.naminorthernnevada.org
@naminorthernnv (Instagram)
Facebook:
http://www.facebook.com/Namiofnorthernnevada

CHOW

CHOW's mission is to support the lives of food/beverage/hospitality workers. A community created by hospitality workers for hospitality workers, we offer education, support and resources to make the industry a safer, saner and more sustainable place for all.

Erin - I am Erin Boyle, CEO of CHOW. Beyond my professional role, I'm a friend, sister, partner, daughter, dog lover, potter, avid reader, crafter, walker, and chef. Trained at the Culinary Institute of America, I've worked in San Francisco, Washington DC, New York, and Denver. After nearly two decades in the industry, I transitioned to teaching, which I found fulfilling.

I've faced my own battles with depression, anxiety, ADHD, and PTSD. Seeking help in 2013, I found a therapist who helped me name and manage my challenges. After witnessing struggles with mental health and substance use among my staff, family, and friends in hospitality, in 2019, I committed to improving access to mental health resources for all. As CHOW's CEO, I focus on outreach, education, and destigmatizing conversations about health in the restaurant industry.

Jasmin- I am Jasmin Vitolo Parks-Papadopoulos, former toxic Chef, currently Certified Life Coach. For years I struggled with High Functioning Anxiety, and it wasn't until I delved deep into my behavioral patterns and life choices, that I could see how my most harmful traits and habits were nestled into the profession I had chosen. A product of the Great Resignation, I came to CHOW in 2020 for support in detaching myself from an industry that I had hidden my discomfort in for so long. I needed to find new ways forward and surround myself with people, like myself, who were struggling to establish their identity and support their mental health. Now as a part of the CHOW team, I am passionate about building an interactive community that extends everyone the accepting and warm welcome I received when joining CHOW. My goal is to increase visibility for our organization and spread the word about our message.

YOUR GO TO
MENTAL HEALTH RESOURCE LIST

741741

CRISIS TEXT LINE
IN A CRISIS? TEXT HOME TO 741741 TO CONNECT WITH A CRISIS COUNSELOR. YOU CAN USE A CRISIS LINE WHEN YOU'RE EXPERIENCING A SITUATION THAT FEELS OVERWHELMING, URGENT, OR POTENTIALLY HARMFUL TO YOURSELF OR OTHERS. YOU CAN ALSO USE A CRISIS LINE TO HELP SOMEONE AROUND YOU.

988

THE SUICIDE & CRISIS TEXT LINE PROVIDES 24/7, FREE AND CONFIDENTIAL SUPPORT FOR PEOPLE IN DISTRESS, PREVENTION AND CRISIS RESOURCES FOR YOU OR YOUR LOVED ONES, AND BEST PRACTICES FOR PROFESSIONALS IN THE UNITED STATES.

(800) 662-4357

SAMHSA'S NATIONAL HELPLINE. SAMHSA'S MISSION IS TO REDUCE THE IMPACT OF SUBSTANCE ABUSE AND MENTAL ILLNESS ON AMERICA'S COMMUNITIES.

WWW.CHOWCO.ORG/RESOURCES

CHOW PRIDES ITSELF ON BEING A RESOURCE BROKER AND WE KNOW THAT FINDING THE RIGHT RESOURCE CAN BE AN OVERWHELMING PROCESS. THAT'S WHY WE'RE HERE! WANT TO HAVE SOMEONE GUIDE YOU THROUGH THE PROCESS IN REAL TIME? CONTACT COMMUNITY@CHOWCO.ORG AND WE'LL GET YOU CONNECTED TO THE RIGHT PLACE.

Contacts: community@chowco.org, www.chowco.org

Social handles:

Instagram @chow_org

Twitter @chow_org

Tiktok @chow_303

LinkedIn https://www.linkedin.com/company/chowco

Facebook https://www.facebook.com/choworg & https://www.facebook.com/groups/choworg

Cooks Who Care

About Cooks Who Care

Cooks Who Care (CWC) is an organization dedicated to supporting the health & well-being of people working in the Food & Beverage Industries. CWC currently focuses their efforts on supporting food service workers and shares profits to mental health partners, Southern Smoke Foundation and The Nava Center. Founders Maria & Scott Campbell are tireless advocates, raising awareness about the mental health challenges specific to their industry peers.
Learn more by following on Facebook, Instagram & at https://chescocf.org/fund/cooks-who-care

Our Mission

The Food & Beverage Industry is in the middle of an on-going mental health crisis. The Covid-19 pandemic brought this situation to the forefront of a national conversation, but the conditions have existed for years. In light of the mental health struggles that many of our friends in the industry have faced recently, we were inspired to do more to help. With the newly launched CWC Community Fund, we are raising money to fund mini grants for food service workers in the Philadelphia area who are in need of mental health support. Our CWC Community Cookbook is a filming cookbook project where we fundraise for this initiative & 100% of proceeds will fund mental health focused grants with vetted nationwide partners.

About the Book:
"Cooks Who Care Community Cookbook: Entertaining for Mental Health (Philly Edition)"

The Cooks Who Care Community Cookbook is a first-of-its-kind cookbook and film project. This book is a compilation of seasonal recipes shared by 25+ chefs, beverage professionals & health experts (most hailing from the Philadelphia area) who are committed to supporting mental health advocacy in the Food & Beverage Industries. Packed with unique tastes & global flavors, it includes home entertaining recipes for cooks of all skill levels. What really sets this project apart is that each recipe is accompanied by an interactive QR code, linking the user to how-to videos from the recipe contributors themselves. Each video was professionally filmed by cinematographer and producer Eric Lovett Jr., and his team at iLovett Films. These demo video give the reader access to step-by-step instructions from experts in their craft. Taste what the city of Brotherly Love has to offer while supporting mental health 100% of proceeds grow a mental health fund for food & beverage workers available nationwide.

www.cookswhocare.org
Social Media: IG / FB @cookswhocare
Contribute to Community Fund: buy books to be shipped or donate to fund
https://chescocf.org/fund/cooks-who-care

Join the Movement: "Keep on Walking" YouTube Series on Mental Health in the Food Industry

I am thrilled to introduce you to "Keep on Walking," an impactful YouTube interview series by Cooks Who Care, in collaboration with Producers, Monetize Philly, and iLovett Films. Our series, focused on the critical topic of mental health in the food industry, is set to expand with three additional filming sites, providing a platform for a total of 72 individuals from the food and beverage sector to share their personal journeys of overcoming mental health challenges.

We invite you to be a part of this initiative by spreading the word among your colleagues and on social media. The series not only sheds light on the resilience within the industry but also serves as a beacon of hope and motivation. By sharing these powerful stories, we aim to create a community that supports mental health within the food and hospitality sector.

We encourage individuals and brands to actively participate by sharing the journey of "Keep on Walking" and contributing to the conversation on mental health in the food industry. Your involvement is crucial in making a meaningful impact and raising awareness.

Join us, share the journey, and let's make a difference together.

Warm regards,

Maria Campbell, MBA
Chef/Founder
Cooks Who Care

Email: chefmaria@cookswhocare.org
Follow on social: @cookswhocare

New Interview Series: "Keep on Walking" by Cooks Who Care

Cooks Who Care, is launching a new YouTube interview series with media partner, Monetize Philly and iLovett Films to co-produce interviews featuring chef, mixologists and hospitality influencers, foodies and more. One time a month rotating guests will share how they *kept on walking* after struggles they overcame which affected or continue to affect their mental health. Although the circumstances were great - to motivate our community, we want to show that it's possible to keep on walking, even if one-step-at-a-time. The purpose is to connect audiences of industry professionals and food & restaurant lovers to the need for mental health support. Set in restaurant locations as the backdrop, this national series will be filmed regionally showcasing restaurant workers, leaders and foodies in a conversational format. We would invite leading and professionals ready to share their story to these scheduled and curated events partnering with brands who want to align with food industry mental health support.

DETAILS
Film Releases: Monthly filming frequency. Weekly releases.
First Filming Location: Rex at the Royal | 1524 South St, Philadelphia, PA 19146
Second Filming Location: Lucky Well Incubator | 990 Spring Garden St, Philadelphia, PA 19123
Filming Partner: iLovett Films, Camera Operator: Sajid Chaudhary of SJC Productions, Set Designer: Big City Little Kitchen
First Guests: Chef David Feola, Claire Trindle, Dominic Condo, Chef Maria Campbell and
Content Shared: Release single interviews weekly into 2024 on LinkedIn Articles 4.5K followers, Instagram 3.7K, Facebook 1.4K, Youtube Channel with over 25.8K views.

Continue to book 1 location with 4 -6 people and have content to release weekly for the 2024 year on above platforms, to grow reach with partners who care and make a bigger grant funding impact.

CWC Maria, founder, to book interview talent, source locations and build a schedule for 2024.
Seeking B2B Sponsorship Partners to connect to CWC audience, elevate brand positioning in mental health and food & beverage landscape.
Media Partner: Monetize Philly | Film Partner: iLovett Films | Mental Health Partner: The Nava Center

Media Partner	Mental Health Partner	Film Partner	Set Design Partner

Restaurant After Hours

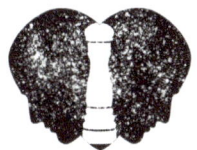

RESTAURANT AFTER HOURS
MENTAL HEALTH RESOURCES FOR THE HOSPITALITY INDUSTRY
501c3 charitable organization

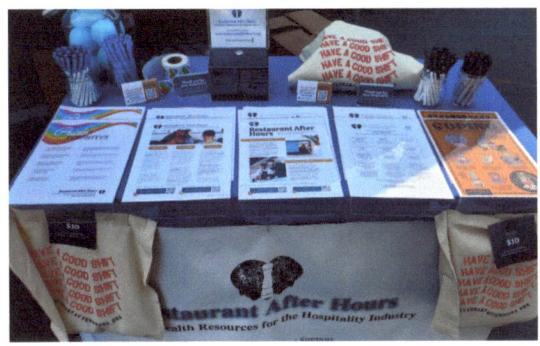

About Restaurant After Hours:

Founded December 28th, 2018 in Brooklyn, NY
501c3 Charitable Organization
EIN 37-1921395
Team consists of 5 Board Members, 1 Executive Director, 1 Director of Mental Health Operations, 1 Outreach Coordinator, and 1 Social Media & Marketing Manager

Restaurant After Hours offers an extensive free-to-use resource list on our webpage. We also offer more direct in-person services along with our advocacy work. We do this on three different levels:

Level 1 - Individual

We work to provide individuals with free and accessible mental health resources and support for hospitality workers. We have an extensive mental health resource list containing 200 resources on our website and are always in the process of adding more. We use these resources for referrals, whether it be for educational purposes, information on joining a support group, or access to free counseling.
We also provide peer support for individuals to help them along their own mental health journeys, as well as for their families who may reach out looking for information on how to support a loved one who may be struggling.

Level 2 - Organizational

We work with restaurant groups and companies to help them understand how to best support their employees with their mental health, and how to optimize their work environment. We have done this by providing mental health training for managers both in-person and virtual, meeting with staff members, and providing presentations at various workplaces. With our workplace partners, we have also aided them with including mental health resources during their onboarding procedures and employee handbooks.

Level 3 - Community

We continually engage with local and international communities to evaluate the efficiency of our work and resources. We connect and partner with other like-minded organizations to maximize our impact, reach, and explore new initiatives together. Some of these organizations include CookzCreed, Ben's Friends, CHOW, HEARD, Not 9 to 5, Cooks Who Care, The Giving Kitchen, Restaurant Workers Community Foundation, Restaurant Opportunities Center United, and many others. Our teams have collectively come together to advocate for a better industry and work environments, and we are frequently putting on panels, presentations, and webinars. We focus on partnering with writers and podcast hosts who have been vital in helping to expand our mission, messages, and outreach. We also set up booths at various events across NYC to personally engage with the community, hand out resources, and have important conversations.

Founder, Zia Sheikh

Zia Sheikh is a born and raised New Yorker and 20-year veteran of the hospitality industry. He learned how to cook at the age of 10 by mirroring his mother in the kitchen. First entering college to pursue engineering, Sheikh followed his passion for cooking and graduated with honors from the culinary and hospitality program at The Art Institute of New York City, which helped him land an externship at The Mercer Kitchen in Manhattan working for Chef Jean-Georges Vongerichten.

Over the course of the next 15 years Sheikh worked in the kitchens of many high-end NYC, New Jersey, and Philadelphia establishments, including being on the opening team of Zahav and 10 Arts by Eric Ripert. In 2007 Sheikh started working as a line cook and manager for the late Chef Floyd Cardoz, who he credits as being his main mentor. Sheikh spent 11.5 years working with Chef Cardoz and they opened four restaurants together, all to critical NYC acclaim.

By 2018 Sheikh recognized working in the industry was taking a massive toll on himself, and the late-night culture of drinking and substance abuse was enabling his addictions. When Sheikh had a near death experience from drinking, he decided to make changes to his life and went on sabbatical for six months to work on his mental health. Upon his return, he started Restaurant After Hours in December 2018, a nonprofit that provides hospitality professionals with mental health education, advocacy, resources, and support.

Zia Sheikh Story (Expanded)

To my fellow hospitality workers and beyond,

In June of 2018 I reached burnout, which is not a word I throw around lightly. After years of never focusing enough on myself, I found myself in a position where both my mental and physical state were completely deteriorated. Between the years of 2016 and 2018, during the opening of my 5th restaurant, the pressure had gotten to me. I was working 80-100 hour workweeks, I was drinking excessively, I had put on 60 pounds, I was always angry, I snapped at staff and belittled the people around me, I lost relationships and never saw my partner. I lost control of myself and my surroundings.

When I was fired from that chef position, I left that exit interview feeling a lot of hope. I decided to take six months off from the industry to focus on myself. I had two goals in mind. I wanted to start therapy, and I wanted to become sober. However, now in a position where I did not have money coming in, let alone insurance, I had no idea where to start. I waived my white flag in a very opening Facebook post to my friends and family, who showed nothing but support. Some provided information on a few available resources, but it still was not enough for what I needed at the time.

I started researching extensively for available resources for people in my position. After a few months, in October, I was able to find a nonprofit in Brooklyn providing five free counseling sessions for anyone who walked through the door, regardless of insurance or job status. They also helped me set up a low-tier insurance, which gave me the opportunity to continue therapy beyond what they were offering. I was diagnosed with having depression, anxiety, substance abuse issues, and disordered eating.

On December 3rd, 2018, I took my last sip of alcohol. I was ready to move on and leave the destructive past behind me. I was ready to put in the work to achieve a healthier and happier future, and most importantly, one that I could remember. The alcohol caused most of my life to be blacked out, memories and timelines I can never get back, all because I did not know how to cope. Individuals turn to alcohol for various reasons, and in my case, it was to hide and suppress all the emotions and trauma during the course of my life which I never spoke about. Cooking started off as solace and an escape from the world, but the systemic cycle of abuse we normalize in this industry, the underlying undiagnosed mental health issues along with the substance abuse, all contributed to my own world being destroyed.

I decided to put an end to the abusive cycle and on December 28th, 2018, I founded Restaurant After Hours, with the intention of helping the many hospitality workers who find themselves in the same position as myself back then.

My passion for this work now can be summed up in two words: "I understand". I will continue to build the organization, the team, the services and available resources, to help the individuals who continually bend over backwards for customers and guests. It's time hospitality workers to care as much for themselves as they do for others, and Restaurant After Hours is here to help.

Chef Zia Sheikh
Founder of Restaurant After Hours

Resources:

Question: What resources have you found helpful?

Answer: Individuals are different, so their mental health journeys are different as well. At Restaurant After Hours, we provide a long list of available and accessible resources because individuals need to find what works best for them. For some this may be a weekly therapy session. For others a support group may work better or working a 12-step program. In some instances, one phone call to a crisis line could provide the information they need.

Navigating these resources is difficult, and the team at Restaurant After Hours is here to support individuals on their journeys. It's very difficult and requires a lot of work, but we encourage individuals to stay hopeful.

Contact Information:
Website: www.restaurantafterhours.org
Email: contact@restaurantafterhours.org
Facebook: Restaurant After Hours, 501c3
Instagram: @restaurantafterhoursnyc

Not 9 to 5

WE ARE NOT 9 TO 5

Not 9 to 5 is a non-profit leader that advocates for improving mental health in the hospitality sector through practical education, meaningful community-building, and resources to break stigma, fuel hope, and advance psychological safety for industry professionals. We collaborate with workers, employers and schools to normalize mental health training, sick leave, workplace accommodations, and healthcare benefits for all segments of the hospitality sector workforce.

RESEARCH & DATA

Pre-pandemic Not 9 to 5 launched our first survey and asked, "Do you experience mental health or substance use challenges?"

90% said yes.

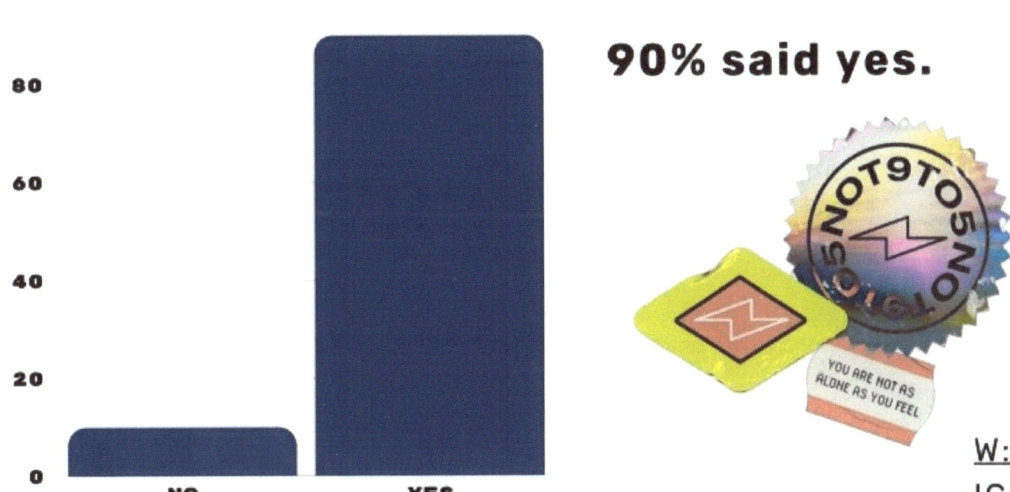

W: not9to5.org
IG: @not9to5_

"THERE IS SO MUCH EMPHASIS ON THE SUSTAINABILITY AND ETHICAL TREATMENT OF THE INGREDIENTS THAT WE USE IN OUR MENUS. WE ARE TRYING TO PUSH US TO HAVE THE SAME FOCUS ON THE ETHICAL TREATMENT OF THE PEOPLE THAT ARE PRODUCING, GROWING, SERVING, AND CREATING EVERYTHING THAT WE CONSUME."

In 2021, with federal funding support Not 9 to 5 launched a research project called Mind Your Health. This global research included exclusively hospitality professionals as participants. In total there were 673 respondents worldwide with the majority in Canada and USA.

These are results from that research, with this percentage of industry folks saying yes to experiencing symptoms of:

- Burnout: 87
- Anxiety: 84
- Depression: 77
- Disordered eating: 63

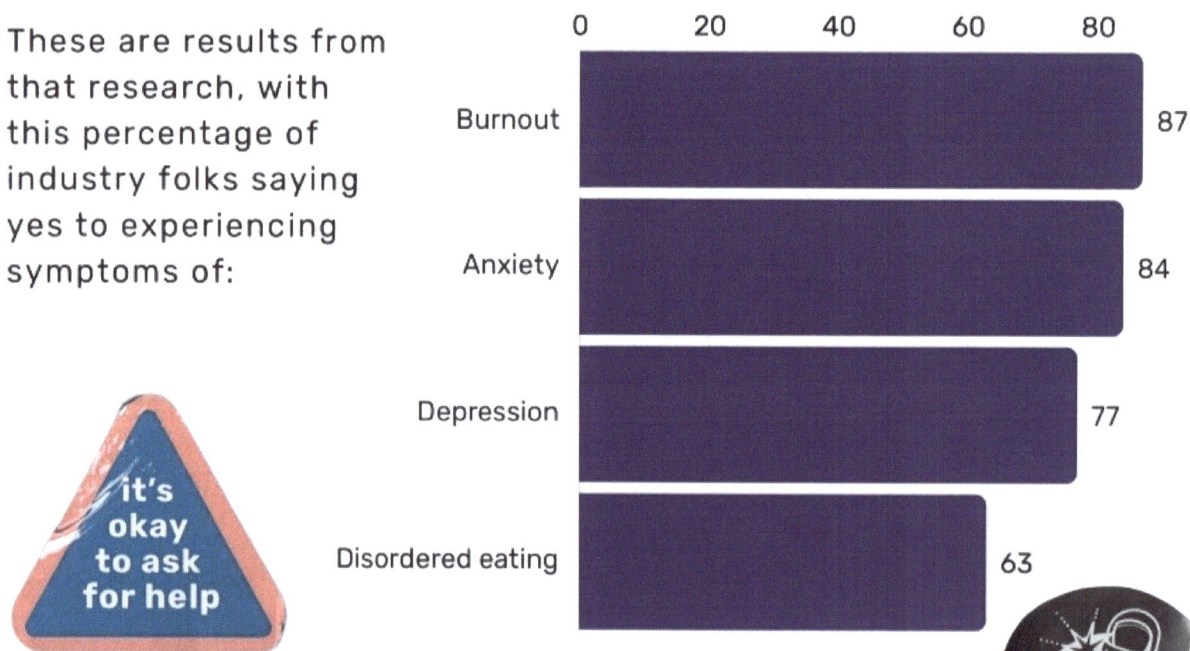

it's okay to ask for help

When asked about speaking openly about mental health in the workplace, 67% say they still "keep it to myself" and try not to let it show.

W: not9to5.org
IG: @not9to5_

Majority of respondents asked for psych education and content to support learning more about workplace mental health. We responded by creating a **workplace mental health certification** called CNECTed. It was designed with an intersectional lens and self-led assessment of learning. CNECTed provides education, training and support skills for employees and employers to operate and work in a psychologically safe workplace. **Use discount code 15OFF for 15% off.**

In addition, Not 9 to 5 produced a critically recognized **short documentary series** featuring an award-winning director and chefs sharing their mental health lived experiences. In addition, we also developed **a podcast called "We Have Lived"** available on Spotify or wherever you listen to podcasts. We Have Lived is an exclusive 14-episode podcast series recorded in sister cities Chicago, USA and Toronto, Canada produced by Not 9 to 5 with creative direction from the Terms of Service Network.

W: not9to5.org
IG: @not9to5_

For those not ready to invest in a course there is now a *NEW* free resource by 7shifts & Not 9 to 5 available.

Hassel Aviles, the Founder and Executive Director of Not 9 to 5, takes you through five lessons:

1. Top Mental Health Concerns in Restaurants
2. Burnout vs. Stress
3. Substance Use
4. Equity and Inclusion
5. Leadership Support

It's all free! Sign up now at **7shifts Academy** or watch on **YouTube** anytime to learn how to support your team's well-being.

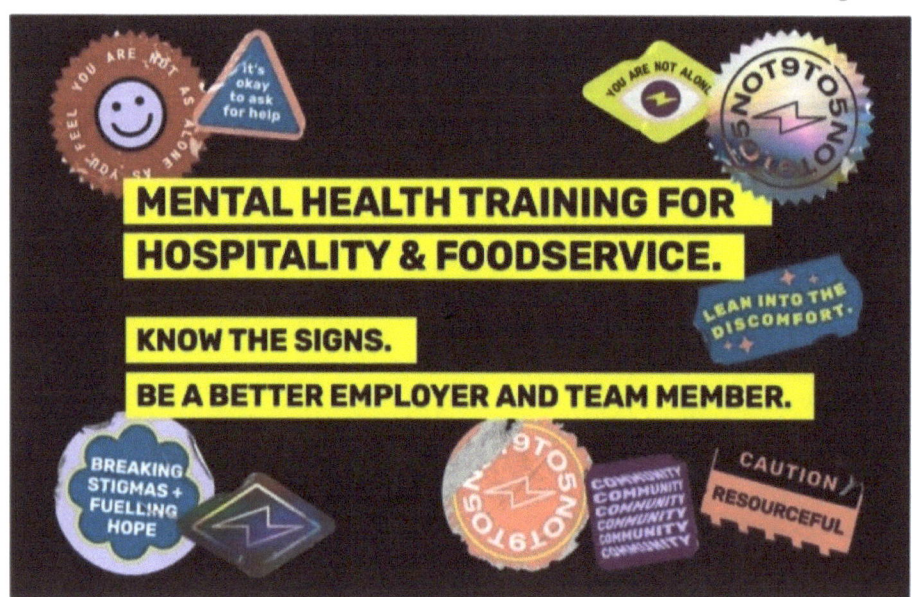

W: not9to5.org
IG: @not9to5_

Winchimes

"Not everyone is built for this journey. Not everyone can observe the spiral we live without becoming dizzy and nauseous themselves. Not everyone is built for this." – Asha Blanchard- Harmon. "Our Mental Illness Will Make It Easy for You To Walk Away". Not My Mental Illness, Blogspot, June 2nd, 2016, https://notmymentalillness.blogspot.com/2016/06/our-mental-illness-will-make-it-easy.html

Established in 2022, Win Chimes is a non-profit organization by Asha Blanchard-Harmon that aims to connect individuals and families grappling with mental health crises to tailored resources and social services. As a single mother of a child with severe mental illness, I personally encountered the hurdles and bias within the intricate support system designed to offer assistance. My family faced continuous challenges, jeopardizing our unity and stability. This struggle motivated me to create Win Chimes, driven by the belief that seeking help should not be an arduous task. It requires significant courage to seek assistance, and I aspire to empower those on the verge of giving up on themselves and their support systems to persevere until things improve.

Win Chimes provides crisis coaching, resources, and educational tools with the mission of not only offering immediate aid but also establishing long-term stability and hope for families in crisis. We aim to assist every family seeking support and become a vital part of their network. By fortifying these connections and delivering ongoing assistance, our goal is to have a lasting positive impact on those affected by mental health challenges. We recognize that hope often acts as a buffer between despair and success, and we are dedicated to offering hope and aid to those in need. Despite our limited resources, Win Chimes has already made a significant difference, and we are steadfast in our commitment to furthering our cause and supporting as many individuals and families as possible.

We don't care what Your history, background, ethnicity, gender politics, social status, income, or any other bias prone features may be. We help anyone who brave enough to ask for our help. Both the individuals grappling with mental health issues and their support networks, collectively experiencing hardship due to mental health crisis and facing their own struggles, are the focus of our services.

Marie Ducksworth, Testimonial and Review

Mon 3/18/2024 9:25 AM

To:Asha Blanchard- Harmon <asha@winchimes.org>

To Whom It May Concern:

I am writing this letter to express my deep gratitude and appreciation for the support and assistance provided by Win Chimes during my family's time of crisis. For the past six months, my family and I have been clients of Win Chimes, and I cannot stress enough how much of a positive impact this organization has had on our lives.

When my husband's mental health crisis left us with no resources or support, I felt hopeless and afraid for the future of my two children and myself. It was during this time that I reached out to Win Chimes, after being referred by a friend.

From the moment we connected with Win Chimes, they provided us with crucial support and resources that helped us stay safe and secure. They helped me secure emergency shelter, permanent housing for my family, connected me with local resources, and even helped my husband get professional help. Additionally, I was able to receive therapy and support for myself and my children, which has greatly improved our well-being.

Most notably, Win Chimes helped us secure a new home with everything we needed to move in and feel comfortable. Without their assistance, I am not sure how we would have been able to get back on our feet and create a stable and safe environment for our family in such a short period of time. I truly believe that without Win Chimes, I may have remained homeless, my children may have suffered emotionally, and my husband's mental health crisis may have been life threatening.

Thanks to Win Chimes, my family and I are on the road to recovery and healing. Their support and guidance has been invaluable during this difficult time, and I cannot thank them enough.

In conclusion, I highly recommend Win Chimes to anyone who may be struggling with a mental health crisis. They truly care about their clients and go above and beyond to provide the necessary support and resources to overcome hardship. Thank you, Win Chimes, for all that you have done for my family and me.

Contact:

909.334.1261 c/t

info@winchimes.org

Web: www.winchimes.org

FB: Win Chimes https://www.facebook.com/winchimesorg?mibextid=ZbWKwL

IG: @winchimesorg

David Manrique

Food As Content™ is a media production and content strategy studio specializing in food and people, with a mission to contribute to a more conscious and inclusive food and media culture that values the planet and nourishes communities.

Founded in 2023 by David Manrique, a New York-based Colombian food photographer, filmmaker, and screenwriter with a background in digital marketing and technology, Food As Content operates under its proprietary Sustainable Food Media Production Framework™, designed to minimize the environmental impact of their productions and to prioritize the benefit of the communities across their value chain.

This framework covers areas such as equipment, sets, transportation, workforce and partnerships, offering business owners, entrepreneurs and organizations in the food space an alternative to stay at the forefront of the digital world, while contributing to a better world for all.

Phone:
347.644.4196

Website:
www.foodascontent.com/home

Instagram:
@foodascontent

LinkedIn:
linkedin.com/company/foodascontent

Pictured above Pastry Chef Francine Tamakloe

5 Simple Actions

to reduce environmental impact when producing content for your food business

In addition to making sure that all the food that you use is edible, and using gloves or tweezers to avoid manipulating the dishes with bare hands, there are simple actions that can help reduce the environmental impact of food waste when producing content for your food business.

Furthermore, keep in mind that what you decide to promote will also have an impact: the carbon footprint of a double burger with brisket is very different from that of a plant-based dish, for example.

Whatever you decide to do, remember to use the opportunity to raise awareness around the importance of reducing food waste to help the planet. Any food content production can be turned into the perfect moment to engage with your community and make a positive impact:

1. Run a social media contest and ask your audience to tag friends that live or work close to your business. Reward new followers with items used for the production.

2. Plan for high traffic hours and offer the items to walk-in customers as a courtesy.

3. Coordinate with a local food pantry or community fridge in the neighborhood where you're located to donate the items after the production.

4. Plan a family meal and turn it into something special for your team and collaborators.

5. Find creative ways to incorporate the leftover food and ingredients into other recipes.

Chef Kimberly Brock Brown, CEPC, CCA, AAC

Kimberly Brock Brown has a journey that has taken her to places – near and far – that would prove important to her career as a culinarian and culinary leader. Raised in the western Chicago suburb, Maywood, Chef Brown attributes her love for cooking to her heritage. Mom was born in Haiti Missouri, Dad was born in Jackson, Mississippi, and the convergence created an appreciation for America's foodways and food people. When it came time to choose geographical paths to pursue career options, the chef left for the Southwest (Dallas) and parts in-between, before settling in Charleston, South Carolina.

Cooking and the love of food, has always been a part of her story.

As the immediate past national president and continuing board member of the American Culinary Federation (ACF), Kimberly Brock Brown has traveled extensively as a representative of the 14,000-member organization. She has been affiliated with ACF since the mid-1980s, rising through the ranks of leadership. Since 2017, she has spoken to culinary students in the United States, the Caribbean and other places overseas. Chef Brown has spoken to women's groups, mainstream groups, small and large audiences about leadership and culinary professionalism. In 2022, she represented ACF at the World Association Of Chefs Society (WACS) in Abu Dhabi.

Among her awards and honors, Chef Brown was inducted into the Honor Society at the National Canadian Culinary Federation in Saskatchewan in 2022 and Honorary Member Saudi Arabian Chefs Table Circle, July 2023 Jeddah Kingdom, Saudi Arabia
. In 2018, she was inducted in the international association of gastronomy, Chaîne des Rôtisseurs, Charleston chapter. And she most recently was selected to serve on the "Kitchen Cabinet" as a chef-leader and advisor, with the likes of José Andrés and other culinarians, for the United States of America's Department of State's American Culinary Corps.

Chef Brown, the citizen, supports the causes of women in leadership, aging and hunger, and culinary entrepreneurship. But in all that she does, she honors the fact that she has been blessed to achieve and receive and counts it as her duty to pay it forward.

Chef Dave Overman

I grew up cooking family meals and helping to prepare large family summer/holiday gathering meals. As a teenager I worked my way up from dishwasher to kitchen steward to banquet sous chef of a summer dinning facility, managing the banquet set up and outdoor turkey and ham live fire roasting pit, at the age of 17 (1983), I quit, professionally cooking, because of the overall stress of dealing with incompetent staff and banquet demands.

Sherry and I were married in 1987, and she had been trained as a "Galley Gourmet Chef" in high school, and she did all of our family cooking.

Around 2000 I started writing, publishing and proofing Dutch Oven recipes, and slowly getting back into cooking as I published more recipes in outdoor magazines.

Around 2013, while having a dinner with my cousin, who had worked his way up from table bussing to Banquet Executive Chef at a 5-star resort, and swapping cooking stories, my youngest daughter Jadynn asked what I was talking about since I seldom cooked at home. I told her that I used to cook a long time ago.

She was a fan of BBQ & cooking competitions on television, and asked me if I could do "that," and I assured her that I could. She then challenged me to "prove it." I told her that I would as long as she came with me.

In 2014 Sherry and Jadynn bout me a BBQ smoker, and I started competing in BBQ competitions, in 2015 I teamed up with Dave Adams of G-Pa D's BBQ, in 2016 I won our way into the World Food Championships in the Steak Category, and we have been competing in World Food Championships every year since; in 2016 I sous cheffed for the 6th place Chili competitor, then in took 4th place in Chicken in 2018 and 10th in Seafood in 2022 (12th in 2000 & 11th in 2023). I have had many memorable wins and losses over the years. One such win came in 2017 as I defeated a long-standing winner and professional chef in the Montana State BBQ Championships Dutch Oven event with a Dutch Oven Beef Wellington presentation; this was the first time that a fellow competitor stated to me "you're just a pedestrian chef."

Dave and I still help coordinate and participate alongside of the Pacific Northwest BBQ Association with feed the Troops at Fairchild Airforce Base, and I still offer catering services and operate a BBQ food truck in Post Falls, Idaho which is open one day per week for "Food Truck Fridays." my food truck is "Hoakie Smoakes," and we offer traditional BBQ food, and some with a twist, custom BBQ sauces, and artisan candied jalapeno peppers and jelly.

As a mostly self-taught home started cook, I take some level of pride in being called a "Pedestrian Chef" by other competitors as it has happened many times since 2017. 😀

Bon appetite,

Chef Likitha Gali

Advisee 2024, James Beard Foundation Legacy Network

Bio:

I am a vegan chef, recipe developer, tester, educator & instructor with experience working as a pastry chef in different cafes & restaurants alongside top pastry chefs like Antonio Bachour, Lara Colman, Avin Thaliath to name a few.

I am currently working as a chef in phoenix, Arizona.

I am the founder of, "The Cheerful Vegan". A vegan cooking & baking blog.

You can find me most of the time in the kitchen working with spices & flavors, incorporating them into my cooking, developing new plant-based recipes & creating beautiful pictures. I am passionate about veganism & plant forward lifestyle which has made a huge impact on me. I have been expanding my skills and knowledge to create more approachable plant forward dishes, for others to experience without the intimidation.

I love to challenge the traditional pastry techniques and create great vegan pastries & desserts. I strongly believe in the beauty of creating not only stunning looking food, but unforgettable flavors. It can turn a very simple dish into an emotion. I like to tell a story with my culinary creations.

My style is simple, bright & airy with a pop of colors. I like to take inspiration from everyday routine, colors, floral foliage, nature, community and create visual stories through pastry & beautiful images with my food photography.

Any projects coming up this year?

This year is very exciting for me. I have been transitioning from pastry chef to vegan chef last year. This year I am launching "The Cheerful Vegan" & re-branding my work & starting my blog, YouTube channel & other social accounts to create a non-judgmental space & community, by sharing amazing recipes, desserts, vegan & sustainable lifestyle, stories with sprinkle of motherhood & inspiration.

Contact Info: Email, social, website.
likitha.pastry@gmail.com
Likitha Gali - on social media
thecheerfulvegan.com is launching soon in April 2024.

Pastry, Resilience & Motherhood
By Chef Likitha Gali

In the bustling pastry kitchen, amidst the aromatic symphony of freshly baked goods, intertwined with the rhythm of life. I, Pastry Chef Likitha Gali, share my journey of resilience, passion and dedication in the world of culinary. Along with juggling to have a delicate balance between demands of career, mental health, womanhood and my role as a devoted mother of two naughty toddlers with unwavering determination and grace.

Each morning, before the sun had even risen, I would slip quietly out of bed, careful not to disturb my two precious boys. I would start my day with a gentle kiss upon their forehead and a heavy heart, preparing myself for another day. Their innocent faces fill me with a sense of purpose, a reminder of the love & joy that fuels me. As I step out of the door, the cool morning breeze on my cheeks reminds me of another day I am blessed & grateful for. With each step I take, I accept the dual roles of motherhood and chef, converging in a delicate balance that requires unwavering commitment & resilience.

Stepping into the kitchen every morning, I embrace my role, as a chef with heart filled with passion and a mind brimming with creativity. Here, amidst the whirring of mixers and the gentle hum of ovens, I find solace — a sanctuary where my culinary prowess knew no bounds. But working in the kitchen comes with its own challenges, highs and lows, triumphs and setbacks. With busy days, long work hours, physical stress & more which can be very hard on the body & mind. Not to forget, challenges of being a woman in the kitchen often dominated by men, determined to carve your own path amidst the chaos. Beneath the facade of confidence lay a silent battle with anxiety and self-doubt, a constant companion on this journey of life.

I reached rock bottom at one point in my life, where I wanted to give up on myself. But I refused to let struggles define me. My journey towards self-discovery and healing began to take shape — a journey marked by courage, resilience, and the unwavering support of loved ones. With the help of therapy, I confronted my mental health struggles head-on — breaking free from the chains of silence and stigma that had once held me captive. Seeking help and support to navigate the turbulent waters of my mind. With each step forward, I grow stronger, more resilient, more determined to conquer my mental & physical health, which threatened to hold me back.

But perhaps the most profound transformation of all was the one that took place within my heart — a transformation fueled by self-love, acceptance, and the unwavering belief that I was deserving of happiness and fulfillment. I took self-love very seriously. It helped me take small steps towards giving myself time, grace & love. Whenever the mom guilt hits me, I tell myself, "Self-Love Is Not Selfish". Instead, it's a way to love myself & give more to everyone around me, let it be at home or work. As I look into the mirror, I reflect back at the moments when I had weathered the storms of life and emerged stronger, wiser, and more empowered than ever before. It's an everyday journey in itself to show up for yourself first.

But amidst all this, I never lost sight of what truly mattered most to me – my family. Despite the long hours and the physical exhaustion that often accompanied at work, I always made time for my two boys. Drawing strength from the unconditional love I shared with my children and the unwavering support of my partner. Showering them with love, affection and laughter I make sure I spend time with them playing, dancing & baking yummy treats. Their smiles lit up her world.

For my kids, I am more than just a chef; a safe place, hope, a symbol of possibility, a supermom capable of turning ordinary moments into extraordinary memories with culinary creations and unwavering love & support, who would move mountains to ensure their happiness and well-being.

Never give up on yourself & the things that matter the most to you. Create some time for yourself & love yourself a little bit more every day.

Chef Tala Hairston

Chef Tala Hairston was born and raised in Bowie, Maryland and spent most of her career working in Washington DC. Born to a Filipino mother and an African American father, she has always been surrounded by food and took an early interest in cooking and experimenting in the kitchen. Family time is centered around shared meals every night. Birthdays, holidays, and gatherings featured favorite dishes and delicacies. She knew early on that she wanted to go to culinary school and one day open her own business.

After graduating from Georgetown Visitation Preparatory School in Washington, D.C., Chef Tala attended Johnson & Wales University and received her Associates Degree in Culinary Arts in 2004. She was immediately hired by the Grand Hyatt Washington Hotel in Washington DC as a cook. This experience exposed her to the full range of banquet, cafeteria, restaurant and off-premise catering service. She learned how to work in a fast paced, high-volume food service environment. In order to further learn the business side of the food service industry, she attended University of Delaware and received her Bachelor's Degree in Hotel, Restaurant and Institutional Management in 2007.

Upon graduation, she landed a three-month management internship with Restaurant Associates, a division of Compass Group, where she learned how to run the front and back of the house operations of a museum café in the Smithsonian Institution, in Washington, DC. At the end of the internship, she was hired as Cash Room Manager at the National Gallery of Art Museum and was quickly promoted to Café Manager. As her career progressed, she branched out and worked as Assistant Manager at Panera Bread and helped open and run the Tenleytown store in Washington DC. Restaurant Associates lured her back when she was offered the position of Supervisor at the National Gallery of Arts.

Chef Tala's big break happened when she was asked to be the Sous Chef at the National Museum of African American History and Culture (NMAAHC) when it first opened in September 2016. Working at the NMAAHC was her first taste of what it was like to be a full time Sous Chef. She quickly had to learn how to run a brand new twelve-million-dollar operation that made all its food from scratch. She knew if she could manage this, she could do anything!

In 2018, Chef Tala accepted the position of Senior Sous Chef at Ginger Cove, a 5-star premier retirement community in Annapolis, Maryland run by Flik. She learned a lot about running a restaurant, menu planning, cooking and serving food to order. She is currently the Sous Chef at the Mitsitam Native Foods Café at the National Museum of American Indian in Washington, DC and a member of Just Call Me Chef and organization for Black female chefs..

Chef Robert Bonner

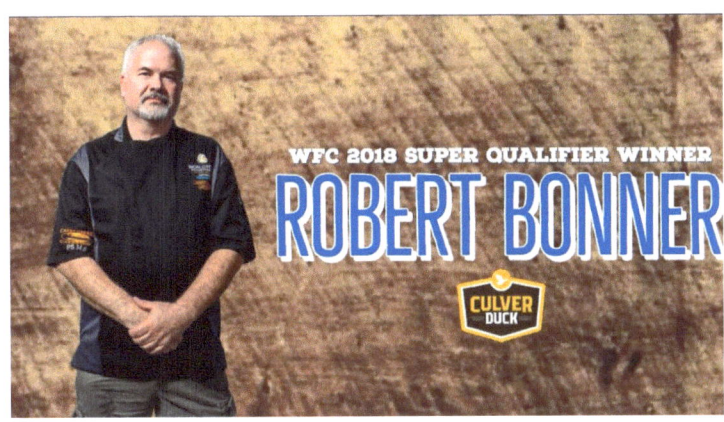

Early on, I saw that food brought people together. In Boy Scouts, my scout master challenged me to cook a Thanksgiving meal on a camp out. The challenge was accepted, and my love of cooking grew. Fast forward to 2015 and bought my 1st food truck. 3 years and 3 food trucks later, decided to branch out to a restaurant. My competitiveness led me to compete in the local Oyster Festival - winning the golden ticket to the World Food championships. Winning 2nd in the Seafood division, I have continued to compete in food cook offs and run the cafe. Though I am still passionate about food, the cafe has given me the ability to support my local community - especially the local Veterans and First Responders.

2017 2nd place World Food Championships Seafood Division
2018 Super Qualifier Culver Duck 1st place
2022 People's Choice Award
2023 6th Place Soup

Chef Terence Tomlin

Chef Terence Tomlin, born and raised in Bridgeport, Connecticut came to the Washington, D.C. Metropolitan area in 2001. Prior to his relocation, Tomlin began his cooking career in 1989 working at The Bridgeport Holiday Inn, The Metropolitan/Bar 45, Tavern on the Green, Shark Bar and other reputable New York tristate restaurants.

After moving to the Washington, D.C. Area, Tomlin worked for the Ritz Carlton in Pentagon City, where he met and trained under Executive Chef Matthew Morrison, who continues to work with Tomlin to this day. Tomlin took a short hiatus from his cooking career to focus on family but returned to open his own restaurant. Although the doors of his restaurant were closed due to a reclassification of the building, Tomlin kept his passion alive and continued his upscale dining education by working at Brian Voltaggio's Range, the Marriott and by assisting the launching of a local creole restaurant.

Tomlin opened Terence Tomlin The Upscale Dining Experience in 2014 and has been instrumental in various high profile personal catering events from Farm to Table, taste of dc events mentoring classes etc. Tomlin and longtime friend Mylie Durham IV from Growroom Productions launched Tomlin Seasonal Sweet Earth Treat Ice Cream and Sorbet which aims to educate consumers on the value and flexibility of creating with vegetables. Tomlin is the former executive chef of Hawthorne rooftop-tavern in Washington,D.C.

Tomlin, with paralysis in his right side won the Maryland Foodie Fest Seafood competition in 2019 and competed in World Food Championship in Dallas,Texas.

Tomlin won The Breaking Bread National Championship in 2021...with one hand.

Tomlin now does fine dining in the Hampton Roads with one hand.

Chef Jonathan Hicks

I like to say I was born in Harrisburg, PA raised in Baltimore, tempered in Providence, RI and figured out how to put all together when I returned home. I am a CHEF. I love to cook, I live to cook. I love the power I have to brightened someone's day with food. Chefs create more than just the food that's on the table, we create moments and memories and I live for that. I'm also a competitive chef and love the thrill of battle. I live my chef life the way samurai did in the past, steel sharpens steel. I love to test myself against the best, and forge friendships and rivalries that push you to unlock new levels. I'm also a Uneek Chef, and what I mean by that is I am teacher, a mentor, an enforcer at times as well. I invest in you, we grow together, to cook and become a real team will force you to connect with people and find out the ways to drive them to the next level.

I'm fiercely loyal to the people that have helped me get to where I am, as a CHEF I can cook yes but to run a restaurant, I know I am nothing without the TEAM. I genuinely believe a CHEF can change lives with more than just food, that's why I have the same core team with me for the last few years. A CHEF inspires the team to work those hard hours, and then the food just reinforces all of those things. FOOD IS An ART; I AM An ARTIST. I love to put on the show, and make a bite, that creates a memory and now we are linked. (that's the power of a Chef, that can use the power of food the right way).

I have been a chef for 18 years (I would be honest and say 10 years I've been a CHEF, I had to figure my powers out), I have been competing for the last 5 years. With that food has taken me to some amazing places and opportunities like Guys Grocery Games, Food Network, World Food Championships, Plate It Local, TV appearances and more. The greatest thing about being a CHEF is the people, I have met and become friends with some of the most amazing people. It's so fulfilling to see someone you worked with elevate to next level. It's powerful to be able to give some a chance to learn a craft that could change their way of life. I AM PROUD TO BE A CHEF, as far as I'm concerned, I have my superpower. I change your day with a plate of food.

Chef Catina Smith

Catina Smith 38, lovingly known as Chef Cat is Baltimore native and chef. Cooking for over 18 years in all facets of the culinary industry. Ranging from small cafes, hotels, universities, catering, and fine dining. Cat graduated from Baltimore International College with a degree in Professional cooking, an Associates degree in Hotel and Restaurant Management, as well as a Bachelor's degree in Organizational Management. Catina is also a Airforce veteran. Chef Cat is the founder of Just Call Me Chef, a culinary sisterhood building relationships amongst Black Women Chefs. This national organization focuses on networking and mentorship. Most recently Catina bought a 3-story building with her partner Kiah Gibian, and converted it into a commissary kitchen, and community hub; that hosts over 26 small food businesses. "Our Time Kitchen" is radically changing kitchen culture, helping small woman owned food business thrive and grow, with women of color in mind. Chef Cat is also on the board of the Food Project a nonprofit in southwest Baltimore for inner city youth, where she aids in the culinary curriculum. She has also started her own cooking class series just for boys, teach them culinary fundamentals, featuring local guest male chefs.

If you want to tap in with Chef Cat she hosts the fine dining dinner series "3 petals" and is also available to hire for intimate catering events.

She has 3 children 15- Isaiah, 14-Micah, and 3- Joshua.

Chef Cat has been named by Baltimore Sun "Women to watch" 2020

Named best Chef is Baltimore by Baltimore Magazine 2020

Black Women in Food Honoree

Winner of "Plated it" Baltimore (cooking competition)

Nominated for Chef of the year for The Restaurant association of Baltimore (2019)

Women Leading Baltimore 2023

And has several features to include:

Baltimore Magazine, New York Times, Bon appetite Magazine, Women's Health Magazine, Cherry Bombe Magazine.

Chef Natasha Waller

WHY AM I HERE

People always ask me, "How long have you been cooking?" I always respond with "Since a child." As a child, I can remember watching Racheal Ray and going into the kitchen to mimic being on television and cooking in front of a live audience. It was amazing. I was not able to buy the specific ingredients Rachael used, but I would always make my favorite things and just practice being a live chef. During the holidays, I would also make my favorite things while no one was looking. The holidays were the times I asked to help out in the kitchen because I knew there would be other people tasting the food that I helped to prepare. My grandmother, Susie, is an amazing cook and I obtained knowledge from her originally. I owe my love for food to her.

Growing up I thought I wanted to be an author. I loved writing, telling stories, and explaining things in great detail. It was a talent that I possessed. I wrote because it made everything that was messed up in my life, great again. Friends, family, events, you name it, I wrote about it. I used to write fictional stories and I shared them with my closest friends. I told them that everything was made up and it is how I wanted my life to really play out. I write a lot of made-up stories but I think it is time that I write about and share my truth.

I am Natasha Shane Waller, born in Hyattsville, Maryland. I attended Bladensburg Elementary, William Wirt Middle, and; Bladensburg High School before moving away to New York to attend culinary school in 2013. In 2015, I studied abroad in Italy for three months and learned the technique and craft of a true Italian chef. Upon graduating and figuring out my place in the world, I fell into a deep dark depression. I was working as a full-time employee at a prestigious hotel in National Harbor, Maryland, but I only had part-time hours. At the age of 24, I was the highest-paid line cook, and that ultimately set me back and caused me to fall into a deeper depression. I gave up on life and what really made me happy. I began to despise the situations of life and humans as a whole. This hate affected my attitude tremendously. After speaking to a chef at my job, I gained my love back. I established PlatesbyPreddie in 2017 and in June 2018, I officially launched PreddieCooks: PlatesbyPreddieCatering and PlannedbyPreddieEvents. In June 2020, we officially became an LLC. This is a memoir of growing up as well as other life experiences as a chef. These are life experiences that I faced which ultimately created the confident chef and overall person that I am today.

I am Chef Preddie. I am Preddie Tash.

This memoir is a collection of previously written poems, stories, and notes experienced by Natasha Waller. These are not fictional stories. They are stories that ultimately made me choose LIFE over Death. From lessons and adventures, I will provide insight into my life and career as a chef from grade school to where I am in life currently.

In June of 2017, I had my first suicide attempt. Today, I am finally able to tell my story in hopes of saving others.

You are Good Enough.
You Deserve to be here.
You are worthy.
You are alive because God has a plan.
You are alive because there is more.

Please Enjoy.

THE TURN AROUND
HOW FOOD HEALED ME

As C-CAP alum Brother Luck once said, "Luck is what happens when opportunity meets hard work." Natasha is the living proof of this.

While cooking is often a casual hobby for a kid, Natasha Waller has always approached the culinary world with a studious passion. Growing up in Hyattsville, Maryland, Natasha would race home from school to watch her idol Rachel Ray, pen and paper in hand to write down each recipe so she could reproduce it. When her grandmother cooked, she would watch her every move and write it all down.

It's no surprise that when Natasha started high school, she immediately enrolled in a nutrition class. As a junior, she was thrilled when she was accepted into the C-CAP program at her school, learning from C-CAP coordinators Yvette Williams and Chef Troy Williams. "Ms. Yvette was constantly busy but she always had time to make sure I had what I needed. If she could be very busy and still get things done, then I knew I could too." Natasha reflected.

As a senior, Natasha won second place at the C-CAP cooking competition, a win that changed her life. She was awarded a full-tuition scholarship to Monroe College, where she has already completed her associate's degree in Culinary Arts and is now working on her bachelor's degree in Hospitality Management.

But Natasha being Natasha, she decided to squeeze a semester abroad in Italy between her two degrees in three years, funding it herself through a crowd-funded campaign. She is a motivated young woman who uses every tool in her arsenal to take full advantage of the opportunities presented to her. If her life thus far is any indicator, we know that her future will be extremely successful.

C-CAP has taught me to be determined and never to give up.

NATASHA WALLER ALUMNA

Food has always been a passion of mine. I graduated in 2016, with a Bachelor's Degree in Hospitality Management and received an Associate in Culinary Arts. I always knew what I wanted to do with my life, however the direction to get there was not planned. In June 2017, I went through my great depression. For months, I gave up on life. I went to work and came home. I was a line cook at Gaylord National from the time I graduated from college up until 2020. My depression started at the Gaylord. Then life as an adult started and I was not ready. Paying bills, finding my own means of transportation along with buying and cooking myself dinner. The change had started to occur. Due to not knowing how life was going to be, I started thinking about my childhood and how things had come to be. My longest relationship was with someone who never really wanted to build a real relationship with me but for some reason we kept trying to make it work. It was not a good situation for me to be in. In order for Natasha Waller to GROW, she had to let go of the toxic influences. She had to own her feelings. She had to positivity after losses. She had to remember WHO TF PREDDIE TASH WAS!

THE TURN AROUND
HOW FOOD HEALED ME

In September 2017, I sold my first plate. By June 2018, I had officially launched PlatesbyPreddie Catering. I had no idea of the direction of this company, but I knew I wanted to cook to be happy. I wanted to create recipes and experiment because it was my one true love. In February 2019, I hosted my first event under PlannedbyPreddie Events. In June 2020 I registered with the State of Maryland and became a LLC officially becoming PreddieCooks,LLC. In August 2020, during a pandemic, I launched Preddies Picnics. December 2022 concluded a very successful year for this brand.

In 2019, I put ME first. I said NO. I did things on my own terms.
In 2020, I quit my toxic job to focus on being a full-time entrepreneur.
In 2021, I was in my healing phase and learned so much about Natasha, Tasha/Tash, and Chef Preddie. I became a Suicide Prevention First Aid Coach
In 2022, I finished this memoir. I traveled as a chef. I gained partnerships as a chef.
In 2022, I hosted a Black Business Brunch, Galantines Brunch, Easter Extravaganza, and Mental Health Expo
In 2023, I am coming so much harder. Thank you to my supporters.

If I can leave you with anything, it is this:

GOD TURNED IT AROUND FOR ME, HE WILL DO IT FOR YOU
YOU SEE THE GLORY, BUT YOU NEVER KNEW THE STORY
I AM ALVE BECAUSE GOD HAS A PLAN
I AM ALIVE BECAUSE THERE IS MORE
IT IS NOT ABOUT WHERE YOU CAME FROM, IT IS ABOUT WHERE YOU ARE HEADED

Chef Keema Johnson

Resource:
Navy Veteran and all-around great resource.
Dr. Kratel Ruiz-Washington
www.psychologytoday.com/us/therspist/kratel-ruiz-washington-vienna-va/486088

Resource:
Self-Love Workbook for Women: Release Self-Doubt, Build Self-Compassion, and Embrace Who You Are (Self-Love Workbook and Journal)

Resource:
The Dialectical Behavior Therapy Skills Workbook: Practical DBT Exercises for Learning Mindfulness, Interpersonal Effectiveness, Emotion Regulation, ... (A New Harbinger Self-Help Workbook)

Resource:
Great for Maryland residents, I'm not sure if they do outside of Maryland. They virtual therapy and psychiatric appointments.
www.safeharborbc.com

Please connect with us:
Website: www.cookzcreefoundation.org
Email: cookzcreedfoundation@gmail.com
Instagram: @cookzcreedfoundation
Facebook: Cookzcreed Foundation

Volume 2:
Elevating Mental Health Mindfulness and A Deeper Dive Into Navigating Chef/Hospitality Challenges.

Coming Soon!!!

BIBLIOGRAPHY

*Note: All statistics/research for states have websites, links, or hyperlinks directly to the site, facility, article, etc.

QUOTES:
Embrace Health
Mental Health Match
Womensday
American Behavior Clinics
Master Center
Mens Health
Brainy Quote
Good Reads

Statistics/Research:
Datamyte
Culinary Health Fund
National Institute of Health
CozyMeal
Xtra Chef
The Mahoney Group
Substance Abuse and Mental Health Service Administration
American addiction Centers
North Jersey Recovery Center
Mental Health America National
National Alliance on Mental Illness
Drug Abuse Statistics
Kaiser Family Foundation
American Foundation for Suicide Prevention
Michelin Guide
Mindful
Psychology Today
Chef With Issues
Food Tank
Food and Wine

GRATITUDE REFLECTION

NAME: DATE:

DESCRIBE WHAT ARE YOU GRATEFUL FOR TODAY
_____
_____
_____
_____

3 THINGS WHAT YOU LOVE ABOUT YOURSELF
_____
_____
_____
_____

THE THINGS YOU CAN APPRECIATE
_____
_____
_____
_____

www.cookzcreedfoundation.com

5 minute journaling

ONE THING I WANT TO REMEMBER ABOUT TODAY...

_____
_____
_____
_____
_____

TODAY I FELT...

_____
_____
_____
_____
_____

TODAY I'M GREATFUL FOR

_____
_____
_____
_____
_____

Favorite Feel Good Recipe

Date ....

Name of Recipe ....

Source ....

.... Time .... Serve ....

INGREDIENTS

....

....

....

....

....

INSTRUCTIONS

....

....

....

....

....

....

MY NOTES

www.ingramcontent.com/pod-product-compliance
Lightning Source LLC
Chambersburg PA
CBHW041832060526
44119CB00105B/227